THE 100+ SERIES™

READING COMPREHENSION

Essential Practice for Advanced Reading Comprehension Topics

Grade 7

Carson-Dellosa Publishing LLC
Greensboro, North Carolina

Credits
Content Editor: Christy Howard
Proofreader: Carrie D'Ascoli

Visit *carsondellosa.com* for correlations to Common Core, state, national, and Canadian provincial standards.

Carson-Dellosa Publishing LLC
PO Box 35665
Greensboro, NC 27425 USA
carsondellosa.com

ISBN 978-1-4838-1577-0
06-341227784

Table of Contents

Introduction

Organized by specific reading skills, this book is designed to enhance students' reading comprehension. The engaging topics provide meaningful and focused practice. The reading passages are presented in a variety of genres, including fiction, nonfiction, and poetry. Subject matter from across the curriculum, including topics from science, history, and literary classics, deepens student knowledge while strengthening reading skills.

The grade-appropriate selections in this series are an asset to any reading program. Various reading skills and concepts are reinforced throughout the book through activities that align to the Common Core State Standards in English language arts. To view these standards, please see the Common Core Alignment Chart on page 4.

Common Core Alignment Chart

Common Core State Standards*		Practice Page(s)
Reading Standards for Literature		
Key Ideas and Details	7.RL.1–7.RL.3	6–7, 10–13, 24, 30–31, 34–39, 42–45, 48, 56–60, 62–67, 77–78, 85, 92–95, 97–119
Craft and Structure	7.RL.4–7.RL.6	6–7, 10–11, 30–31, 34–39, 58–59, 62–67, 74, 76–78, 81–82, 111–118
Integration of Knowledge and Ideas	7.RL.7–7.RL.9	6–7, 10–11, 24, 30–31
Range of Reading and Level of Text Complexity	7.RL.10	12–13, 24, 38–39, 44–45, 56–57, 60, 62–63, 74, 76–77, 80–81, 85, 92–95, 97–110, 116–117
Reading Standards for Informational Text		
Key Ideas and Details	7.RI.1–7.RI.3	5, 8–9, 14–23, 25–29, 32–33, 40–41, 46–47, 49–55, 61, 68, 70, 79, 83–84, 86–91, 96
Craft and Structure	7.RI.4–7.RI.6	5, 8–9, 14–23, 40–41, 46–47, 69, 71–72, 75, 80, 86–87, 90–91
Integration of Knowledge and Ideas	7.RI.7–7.RI.9	5, 30–31, 40–41, 86–87
Range of Reading and Level of Text Complexity	7.RI.10	5, 8–9, 14–15, 18–19, 25, 28–29, 32–33, 49–55, 61, 68–73, 79–80, 83–84, 86–91, 96
Writing Standards		
Text Types and Purposes	7.W.1–7.W.3	12, 13, 40, 41, 106, 107
Range of Writing	7.W.10	12, 13, 40, 41, 106, 107
Language Standards		
Vocabulary Acquisition and Use	7.L.4–7.L.6	8–9, 20–23, 36–39, 42–43, 46–47, 58–60, 64–82, 92, 98–103, 112–115, 118–119

Name_______________________________

Read the passage. Then, answer the questions.

Understanding Bullying: It's Never Okay

Many students are bullied on school grounds every day. Sometimes bullying happens in the classroom, the cafeteria, the playground, or the school bus. Internet or cyber bullying is also a growing form of bullying. Bullying is aggressive behavior by someone in power. This person uses their power to make someone else repeatedly feel bad, often in embarrassing situations.

Verbal bullying can include teasing someone else, calling someone names, or threatening to hurt him or her. Social bullying is another form of bullying. This type of bullying often takes place as students leave each other out of games or activities, spread rumors about people, or embarrass them in public. Sometimes bullying goes beyond words and becomes physical. Sometimes students are bullied by being tripped, hit, or kicked.

It is never okay to bully someone. Even though it may be hard, students who are bullied should ask for help. Often, students feel helpless or are afraid that the bully may further harm them if they tell an adult and they don't want the behaviors to get worse. If you know of someone who is bullied, you can help them by telling an adult or encouraging them to find positive ways to stand up for themselves.

1. What is the main idea of this passage? in Word

____

2. What are three types of bullying mentioned in "Understanding Bullying: It's Never Okay"?

____

3. What is the author's purpose for writing this text? How do you know?

____

____

____

Name________________________________

Main Idea

Read the passage. Then, answer the questions on page 7.

With the Guys

(1) Hi, my name is Mark. When I left the cafeteria this afternoon, I headed for the gym. It's where I usually hang with my friends. Tavaris and Nick and the guys shoot hoops, or sometimes we just talk. Well, this time we were just talking a bit, nothing special, ya know. That's when Josh came up.

Joshua Lewis is a bit of a loner. He's a nervous kinda guy, always rubbing his arms and legs. Always pushing his glasses back in place. Always on the outs with us kids. Easy to push around. Nick called him the Lone Ranger, and Nick's right.

"Hey, ya guys. Watcha doin'?" Josh says.

"Nothin'." That's Tavaris.

"Shove off, Josh."

"Yeah, beat it."

(2) Joshua just hangs by. He waves his arms like some spastic bird and rubs both shoulders. Looks away like he's going somewhere, right? But he has no place to go. Not really.

"Hey, you deaf, Lewis?" sneers Nick. "Get away, man. You stink!"

Nick muscles over to him, gets his paw on Josh's chest, and shoves. Joshua stumbles a little but doesn't fall. He just pushes up his glasses and eyes Nick nervously.

Some girls giggle. No one speaks for Joshua. We just nod. We're cool.

"Go find Silver, Lone Ranger," says one kid.

"Yeah, giddyup, little doggie," Nick goes.

Joshua's got a red face by now. He's always getting that way. He's shakin' like one of those string puppets, ya know? He actually stares at Nick with a kind of scowl. And the kids, we all say, "Oooh!" And then he scratches his hands, and wrinkles his nose, and galumps off toward the classrooms even though we've got another ten minutes, 'least.

"Man, he's easy!"

The guys laugh. We get talkin' about other stuff. Just waitin' til class starts up. Yeah, we're all one happy family.

(3) But I don't know. I mean, when I'm with the guys, I laugh with them. And they're like my family, ya know?

That's what I tell myself. But it doesn't do it right for me. I feel, oh I don't know, like maybe we shouldn't a' messed with Joshua like that. That pickin' on him brings us down too.

I useta read. Ya know? Stuff about knights and lords and soldiers. Bravery and courage stuff. It was lame, right? But maybe it's more honest than this.

Name________________________

Use the passages on pages 5 and 6 to answer the questions.

1. What is the main idea of the first section of "With the Guys"?

____

2. What is the main idea of the second section?

____

3. What is the main idea of the third section?

____

4. Describe the four characters using these words: bully, followers, isolated, and thoughtful.

Mark ____________________ Nick ____________________

Other students ____________________ Joshua bully

5. What do you think would be two possible solutions to making this situation better?

a. ____

b. ____

6. Compare and contrast "Understanding Bullying: It's Never Okay" and "With the Guys." How does each author present information on bullying? How are the passages similar? How are they different?

____

____

____

____

7. How does the author of "With the Guys" use a fictional story to teach a lesson about a real world topic?

____

____

____

Name________________________________

Main Idea

Read the passage. Then, answer the questions on page 9.

Mealtime Manners

What do you think your parents would say if, at your next Thanksgiving dinner, you took a handful of turkey from the platter and crammed it into your mouth? What if you then used the serving spoon to eat some dressing and took your grandmother's glass of water and used it to wash down your mouthful? Of course, they would be horrified, but this style of eating would actually be true to tradition. The Pilgrims, celebrating their first Thanksgiving dinner with their Native American friends, probably ate in just such a manner.

Today, most people in Western cultures expect to eat meals with their own set of silverware, their own plate, and their own glass. Diners use plates to hold their food and drink only from their own glasses. But Europeans did not always eat this way.

In the 1500s, members of the ruling classes used knives to carve helpings of meat. Since they rarely had their own plates and bowls, they would eat the slice of meat off the tip of the knife. They would use shared spoons to eat soup and would dip bread or their fingers into serving bowls of gravy or stew. If a person was rich enough to own a spoon or knife, he or she would carry these to a banquet and use them instead of their hands. There were a few rules for eating behavior. It was considered rude to taste something from a spoon if it was being passed down to another diner. If you had a bone left in your hand after eating a chicken leg, you were expected to toss it politely under the table.

The working poor had even fewer mealtime manners, since they were usually just worried about getting enough food each day to survive. Their main utensils were their hands. When Europeans, such as the Pilgrims, settled in the New World, they brought this eating style with them. They used pieces of bread as spoons for soup, used their fingers for other food, and passed a shared cup at meals.

While the colonists were sharing cups and dipping their fingers into bowls of food, European royalty and nobility were starting to expand their tableware. They were also developing manners to go with their new knives, forks, spoons, plates, and napkins. They started to think of sharing cups or platters as unsanitary and even rude. Their new manners set them apart and underscored their status as an upper class. By the 1700s, these new customs had spread to wealthy American settlers. As new landowners, they wanted to have a higher status than they would have had in Great Britain. They bought their own dishes and silverware and brought them to the colonies.

By the late 1800s, mealtime manners had changed for everyone. As the American middle class grew, so did their demand for tableware that showed off their prosperity. There was also an elaborate system of etiquette or manners by this time. This new emphasis on behavior extended to every aspect of everyday life.

And what about the 21st century? Do our manners continue to become more complex? Just the opposite seems true. We eat fresh fruit and raw vegetables by hand, along with cheese and crackers. We buy burgers and fries at a fast-food restaurant and eat them in the car. We use our hands to eat pizza and tacos. Mealtimes are becoming more casual all the time.

Name________________________________

Use the passage on page 8 to answer the questions.

1. What is the main idea of this story?

____

2. Choose the supporting detail for this sentence: "There were a few rules for eating behavior in the 1500s."

   A. It was considered rude not to use a napkin.

   B. European royalty started to expand their tableware.

   C. You were supposed to toss any bones under the table.

   D. There was an elaborate system of etiquette for banquets.

3. Why did landowners in colonial America buy silverware and dishes?

   A. They wanted to eat more neatly and not spill as many things.

   B. They wanted to prove they had a higher status than they would have had in Great Britain.

   C. They wanted to become members of royalty.

   D. They wanted to have more sanitary eating conditions in their homes.

4. What is ironic about mealtime manners in the 21st century?

   A. After developing a system of table manners, we are starting to eat by hand again.

   B. We are starting to share cups and plates again.

   C. After importing a lot of dishes and silverware, we have worse manners.

   D. We are eating like the Pilgrims, even at Thanksgiving dinner.

Match the vocabulary words to their meanings.

5. ________	status	A. manners
6. ________	etiquette	B. silverware
7. ________	elaborate	C. unclean
8. ________	utensils	D. rank
9. ________	unsanitary	E. complicated or complex

Name________________________________

Main Idea

Read the passage. Then, answer the questions on page 11.

A Lesson in Manners

Thursday is spaghetti night and I couldn't be more excited. I spend all of my fourth-period class thinking about the aroma of Mom's homemade sauce. I always want to help with the meatballs, but she tells me it's her special recipe and I'm not old enough to know the family secret.

As I walk in the house after soccer practice, my mouth waters at the smell of garlic bread. I can hardly wait to eat! I rush to wash my hands as mom calls papa down to eat dinner. I immediately dig in. I can't eat it fast enough. I slurp the noodles and pick up the meatball that fell off my fork and pop it in my mouth.

All of a sudden I realize that both of my parents are staring at me. I can't figure out why, until I look at my fingers and see the sauce dripping from my thumb.

"Young lady, you will not eat spaghetti with your fingers. In addition, you will not slurp your noodles," Mom says sternly.

"Were you raised by wolves?" Papa asks.

"Is this how you eat when you visit your friends?" Mom inquires.

All of a sudden, I feel a twinge of guilt, but then I remember what I learned in social studies class.

"If I lived in Europe in the 1500s my manners would be perfectly acceptable," I tell them. "And the pilgrims probably ate with their hands too! After all, having silverware was once a privilege held by the wealthy. It wasn't until the late 1800s that silverware was common in many households."

I proceed to tell my parents that many people used bread as a spoon hundreds of years ago. I model for them as I scoop up sauce and a part of a meatball on my garlic bread. Mom and Papa are not amused.

"Mia, you are not living in the 1500s or the 1800s and your history lesson does not excuse your horrible manners," my mom explains. "There is no time travel. You live in the 21st century and you will not eat with your hands, ever."

I want to tell her that now, in the 21st century, we do eat with our hands. We eat burgers and fries, and fruits and vegetables, but I don't. Her cheeks are red and her eyebrows are raised. I know she will think I'm being a know-it-all. So I avoid the opportunity for a lesson on 21st-century eating habits. I apologize profusely to both of my parents. I slow down and savor the taste of my favorite meal as my father changes the subject and asks me about my day. In the back of my mind I'm hoping they will ignore me just for a moment, so I can scoop up my last meatball with the last bite of my garlic bread.

Name________________________________

Use the passages on pages 8 and 10 to answer the questions.

1. What is the main idea of "A Lesson in Manners"?

____

2. How does the author let us know how Mia feels about her eating habits?

____

____

3. How does the author let us know how Mia's parents feel about her eating habits?

____

____

4. Does Mia respect her parents? How do you know?

____

5. Compare and contrast "Mealtime Manners" to a "Lesson in Manners."

____

____

6. How does the author of "A Lesson in Manners" use fiction to teach a lesson about manners?

____

____

7. Survey your classmates. Create a list of manners they have been taught over the years. Write a summary about the manners you think are most important.

____

____

____

____

____

Name____________________________________

Main Idea

Read the passage. Then, answer the questions on page 13.

Family Tree

"How did Grandma and Grandpa meet each other, Mom?" asked Sasha.

"I didn't know you were interested in that old stuff," her mother replied, smiling. "They met in 1936. They helped out on the same farm after school. Grandma didn't have many friends at the time."

"What were Grandma's mother and father named?" asked Sasha.

"Their names were Regina and Gerald Bauer," said her mother. "Gerald was the first person in his whole family to be born outside of Germany. That was in 1885. His family had been in the United States for four years when he was born."

Sasha was impressed. "Wow, that was a long time ago. How do you know about all this?"

"For the past few years, your uncle and I have been researching our family history," her mother answered. "We have reconstructed a family tree that goes all the way back to 1749."

"A family tree? What kind of tree is that?" asked Sasha, getting a little confused.

"It's not a real tree, honey," was the answer. "Here, look at this."

Sasha watched her mother draw lines and write names on a piece of paper. She told Sasha a few stories about her ancestors: how her great-uncle had fought in World War I, how her great-grandmother learned English from a neighbor, and how her grandfather had started his business. Sasha was amazed at how interesting their lives were.

"Please tell me more," Sasha pleaded.

Name____________________________________

Use the passage on page 12 to answer the questions.

1. From what country were some of Sasha's ancestors?

   A. Mexico

   B. Poland

   C. Germany

   D. England

2. Sasha's great-grandfather was the first person in his family to

   A. leave Germany.

   B. be born in Germany.

   C. be born outside of Germany.

   D. work on a farm after school.

3. Why hadn't Sasha's mother told her family stories before?

   A. Family histories are only for adults.

   B. She thought that the stories were too sad to tell.

   C. She thought that Sasha was too young to hear the stories.

   D. She did not know that Sasha would be interested.

4. Sasha probably will

   A. ask to hear more stories about her ancestors.

   B. quickly grow tired of the family stories.

   C. write a letter to her grandparents.

   D. ask a friend to tell her family stories.

5. Which statement about Sasha is supported by the text?

   A. She is not interested in past events.

   B. She likes to hear made-up stories.

   C. She is mainly interested in herself.

   D. She seems to like learning about new things.

6. What is the main idea of this story?

   A. A girl learns about her ancestors for the first time.

   B. A girl has just moved to the United States from Germany.

   C. A girl works on a farm along with her mother.

   D. A girl helps her mother research their family tree.

7. Research important facts about your family history. On a separate sheet of paper, write a short story about your family.

Name________________________________

Read the passage. Then, answer the questions on page 15.

When Lightning Strikes

What was Benjamin Franklin thinking when he flew a kite in a thunderstorm? Didn't he realize that his kite could attract a lightning bolt capable of killing him? The Philadelphia inventor was actually very lucky. A bolt of lightning heats the surrounding air to a temperature that is five times the heat on the surface of the sun. Yet the charge is so brief that people can sometimes survive a stroke of lightning. The bolt that hit Franklin's kite was weak. It struck a pointed wire attached to the kite, traveled down the kite string, and ignited a spark at the key that was fastened to the end of the string. With this experiment, Franklin proved that lightning is actually electricity.

Later in his life, Franklin invented the lightning rod, a device that sends lightning's electricity from a rod to a cable in the ground. Lightning rods are still in use today, and are especially handy in places like Florida, where an average of 90 lightning-producing storms hit per year. By contrast, the West Coast receives an average of only three thunderstorms per year.

When a thunderstorm hits, don't be outdoors flying a kite! In fact, it's dangerous to be outdoors at all. The best place to be is inside a building. When lightning strikes a house, it travels through the wires inside the house and then goes into the ground. People in the house are usually protected. People in cars are also fairly safe. If lightning strikes a vehicle, the charge usually travels through the metal frame, bypassing the people inside. If you get caught outdoors, stay away from trees—lightning will strike the tallest object. It's better to crouch in a ditch or a low spot in the land. Stay away from tents, unwired buildings such as old barns, and shallow caves. Bodies of water should also be avoided during a thunderstorm.

Lightning literally bombards the Earth: there are more than 100 lightning strikes every second. In the United States, more people are killed by lightning than by tornadoes or hurricanes. However, nearly twice as many people who are struck by lightning survive than die. Some people have even survived multiple lightning strikes, such as Virginia park ranger Roy C. Sullivan. He was struck by lightning seven times.

So, is lightning nothing but menacing? Actually, lightning plays an important part in the balance of nature. It returns negative energy to Earth and produces nitrogen compounds that are important for plants. There is no reason to panic over lightning. The chances of being killed by a lightning strike are less than one in 2.5 million. So the next time there's a thunderstorm, put away your kite, find a safe place, and enjoy one of nature's most dramatic shows.

Use the passage on page 14 to answer the questions.

1. Describe what "When Lightning Strikes" is about.

____

____

____

2. For what audience did the author write this passage?

____

3. Why do you think that the author started the passage with a reference to Benjamin Franklin?

____

____

4. Does the author present both the negative and positive aspects of lightning? Give examples.

____

____

____

5. Why does the author end the passage with a reference to a kite?

____

____

6. What is the author's purpose in presenting safety tips concerning thunderstorms?

____

____

7. What does the author say are your chances of being killed by lightning?

____

Read the passage. Then, answer the questions on page 17.

The Young Life of Frederick Douglass

I have never met with a slave who could tell me how old he was. Few slave-mothers know anything of the months of the year, nor of the days of the month. They keep no family records, with marriages, births, and deaths. They measure the ages of their children by spring time, winter time, harvest time, planting time, but these soon become undistinguishable and forgotten. Like other slaves, I cannot tell how old I am. This destitution was among my earliest troubles. I learned when I grew up that my master—and this is the case with masters generally—allowed no questions to be put to him, by which a slave might learn his age. Such questions are deemed evidence of impatience, and even of impudent curiosity. From certain events, however, the dates of which I have since learned, I suppose myself to have been born about the year 1817.

...The dwelling of my grandmother and grandfather had few pretensions. It was a log hut, or cabin, built of clay, wood, and straw. At a distance it resembled—although it was much smaller, less commodious, and less substantial—the cabins erected in the western states by the first settlers. To my child's eye, however, it was a noble structure, admirably adapted to promote the comforts and conveniences of its inmates. A few rough, Virginia fence-rails, flung loosely over the rafters above, answered the triple purpose of floors, ceilings, and bedsteads. To be sure, this upper apartment was reached only by a ladder—but what in the world for climbing could be better than a ladder? To me, this ladder was really a high invention, and possessed a sort of charm as I played with delight upon the rounds of it. In this little hut there was a large family of children; I dare not say how many. My grandmother—whether because too old for field service, or because she had so faithfully discharged the duties of her station in early life, I know not—enjoyed the high privilege of living in a cabin, separate from the quarter, with no other burden than her own support, and the necessary care of the little children, imposed. She evidently esteemed it a great fortune to live so. The children were not her own, but her grandchildren—the children of her daughters. She took delight in having them around her, and in attending to their few wants...

Living here, with my dear old grandmother and grandfather, it was a long time before I knew myself to be a slave. I knew many other things before I knew that. Grandmother and Grandfather were the greatest people in the world to me; and being with them so snugly in their own little cabin, knowing no higher authority over me... for a time there was nothing to disturb me. But as I grew larger and older, I learned by degrees the sad fact that the "little hut" and the lot on which it stood, belonged not to my dear old grandparents, but to some person who lived a great distance off, and who was called by Grandmother, "Old Master." I further learned the sadder fact that not only the house and lot, but that Grandmother herself (Grandfather was free) and all the little children around her, belonged to this mysterious personage.

Excerpted from *My Bondage and My Freedom* by Frederick Douglass (Modern Library, 2003)

Name________________________________

Use the passage on page 16 to answer the questions.

1. What reasons does Douglass give for slaves not knowing their ages?

2. Why didn't Douglass initially realize he was a slave?

3. What does Douglass call a high invention?

4. How was Douglass's grandfather different from his grandmother?

5. What year does Douglass think he may have been born?

6. How does the author organize ideas in the text?

7. How can the reader tell this is an autobiography?

Name________________________________

Read the passage. Then, answer the questions on page 19.

A Soldier with a Secret

Among the hundreds of Civil War soldiers buried in Chalmette National Cemetery lies one soldier with a tombstone that reads "Lyons Wakeman, N.Y." If you researched Lyons Wakeman, you might think at first that he was an ordinary soldier of the time. He wrote home to his parents, telling about battles and marches. He described what it was like to march 200 miles (321.87 km) in 10 days, and how it felt to experience the heat and humidity of the South for the first time. In one letter, he wrote, "I don't know how long before I shall have to go into the field of battle. For my part, I don't care. I don't feel afraid to go." The soldier did not die from a wound in battle, but from a lengthy illness in 1864.

For years, his New York family did not speak much of Lyons Wakeman. It was not until a great-nephew found the soldier's letters that a well-kept secret was revealed: Lyons was actually a woman. Her name was Sarah Rosetta Wakeman. Her parents, ashamed of Rosetta's "unfeminine" nature, had hidden her letters and tried to allow her younger siblings to forget about her. Rosetta had served in the military and was buried in a soldier's grave without her secret ever being revealed to those who knew her as a private in the Army. And she was not alone. Research has shown that at least 400 women dressed as men to serve in the war, and there may have been many more. These women had different reasons for joining the Army. Some wanted to be with husbands or brothers. Some wanted to fight for the cause of freeing the slaves or protecting the Confederacy. Some wanted adventure.

Rosetta was born in 1843, the first child of a large farming family. Her letters reveal that she wanted to earn more money for her financially struggling family. She left home in August of 1862 and found work on a coal barge. She wrote home and sent part of her pay with every letter. On a trip up the river, Rosetta met a group of soldiers from the 153rd Regiment of New York State Volunteers. They encouraged the "boatman" to enlist. Rosetta was paid an enlistment bonus of $152, which was more than a year's wages for most men of the time. She continued to send home her Army pay until her death, and her reports to her parents speak of her pride in being able to drill, march, and fight as well as any man with whom she served.

If you are thinking that someone should have noticed that Rosetta was short, beardless, and had a higher voice than most men, you are both right and wrong. Rosetta was described in her enlistment papers as being "five feet tall, fair complected, with brown hair, blue eyes, and an occupation of boatman." By the time Rosetta enlisted, the army was routinely accepting younger men and even boys. Smooth skin, shortness, and higher voices were common and gave no cause for suspicion. If her fellow soldiers thought that "Lyon" had a secret, they would assume he was a young teen who had lied about his age...not that she was a farm girl who had decided to earn a man's wages.

The Civil War was full of tragic losses and stories of bravery on both sides of the battle. Perhaps more stories will come to light about the special bravery of women like Rosetta who were determined to fight alongside men in this historic struggle.

Name______________________________

Use the passage on page 18 to answer the questions.

1. What are some of the reasons women decided to join the army?

2. What did Wakeman do with the money she earned?

3. What did Wakeman write about in letters to her parents?

4. How was Wakeman's secret revealed?

5. What is the author's opinion of Wakeman?

6. On a separate sheet of paper, write a summary of the events of Sarah Rosetta Wakeman's life. Be sure to include any details of her early life and her reasons for leaving home.

Name________________________________

Read the passage. Then, answer the questions on page 21.

Remarkable Rooms

You may find more comfortable surroundings, but it would be hard to find more unique overnight stays than in these four loony lodgings.

The first hotel on our tour is Jules' Undersea Lodge, named after Jules Verne who wrote *Twenty Thousand Leagues Under the Sea*. This two-room lodge is anchored to the floor of a lagoon in Key Largo, Florida. Once an underwater mobile research lab, it was converted into a hotel in 1986. Because its entrance can only be reached by scuba diving, guests can pack only the necessities in one small, waterproof suitcase. Televisions in the rooms play only water-themed videos, such as *The Little Mermaid* or *Splash*. The hotel actually has room service and its own chef. If you order a pizza for dinner, a hotel employee will dive down to your room with a large pepperoni-and-cheese in a watertight container.

If an underwater adventure doesn't appeal to you, let's move on to the Ariau Jungle Hotel in Brazil. All of the 138 rooms in this spacious hotel are built on stilts and touch the treetops of the Amazon rainforest. One room sits atop a tree on the banks of the Rio Negro. It can be reached only by boat. Guests can swim in a pool, play in a game room, or go on searches for alligators and piranhas. In your room, monkeys swinging past your windows will entertain you. Be sure not to feed these **treetop acrobats** or your room will be overrun with them!

For the budget-minded, a Japanese capsule hotel is the place to go. These rooms resemble microwaves from the outside; a small door swings outward. The inside is only several feet wide and about six feet (1.8 m) long. You crawl into your room at night, right onto your bed, which takes up the entire floor. You can sit, but not stand. Providing inexpensive nights of sleep for commuters who miss their train home to the suburbs, these hotels are also used for business travel. Each **capsule** has a television and a radio. There's no room service, but you can buy food from vending machines in the lobby.

The Ice Hotel in Jukkasjarvi, Sweden, is our last stop. It's made entirely of ice and snow. The rooms are not heated. Even the beds are made from snow, frozen into solid rectangles. For warmth, each guest is given reindeer skins and a sleeping bag. This frozen accommodation melts each spring and then is reconstructed every fall. Guests go dogsledding or join snowmobile safaris. The hotel's dining room features salmon soup and roasted reindeer. You should plan on bringing a coat, gloves, and a hat to this icy restaurant!

Name______________________________

Use the passage on page 20 to answer the questions. Cite evidence from the text to support your answers.

1. What is the author's purpose for writing this passage?

2. In the third paragraph, to what do the *treetop acrobats* refer?

3. If you stayed in Jules' Undersea Lodge, how would you get a pizza for dinner?

4. What does *capsule* mean?

5. What is unique about the Ice Hotel in Sweden?

6. At which one of the four hotels in the story would you choose to stay? Be sure to describe the reason for your choice.

Read the passage. Then, complete the activities on page 23.

Walls of Water

After a quiet night of fishing in 1896, the Japanese fishing crew set sail for their village. As the shoreline came into view, they were stunned by what they saw. The village lay in a heap. It looked like a giant had come and pounded the houses flat, then tossed them in all directions.

In a sense, a giant had paid a visit. A giant wave called a *tsunami* caused the devastation. It killed roughly 22,000 people up and down the coastline of Japan on that night in June more than a century ago. But this was far from an isolated incident. Tsunamis have stormed like angry monsters in many places around the globe, from New Guinea to the United States. What causes these great sea waves?

A tsunami can occur after an earthquake, an underwater landslide, or a volcanic eruption. Large volumes of water are displaced and form into columns of water. The name, tsunami, means "harbor wave." At sea, the waves are not usually a problem. But when a tsunami reaches shallow water, like a harbor, it can build to an enormous height before crashing into the shore. Some of these waves look like four-story buildings. They are also fast; a tsunami can travel as fast as a jet airplane.

People have little warning when tsunamis hit. In the Pacific Rim countries, the population knows to be cautious after an earthquake or volcanic activity. But an underwater landslide is hidden, like a secret, until the tsunami that it causes moves toward shore. Underwater shelves, like terraces in a field, form where rivers empty into an ocean. Seismic activity can cause the shelf to crumble. The loose sediment cascades down like an avalanche. A tsunami can result from the displaced water.

Japan is the unlucky recipient of the most tsunamis. Next are Chile and Hawaii. United States citizens often have felt the power of these gigantic waves. In 1958, a couple named Bill and Vivian Swanson were fishing on a trawler in an Alaskan bay. At ten o'clock, they felt the boat deck shake and saw a rock avalanche shower down from a nearby mountain. The rocks roared into the bay like a herd of buffalo. The resulting wave was taller than the Sears Tower in Chicago and moved toward their boat at a speed of 100 miles an hour (161 kmh). It flung the trawler to its crest, snapping its anchor line. Miraculously, air formed like a bubble inside the bow of the boat, giving the Swansons just enough time to escape.

Since 1900, more than 380,000 people have lost their lives to these disastrous waves. Because tsunamis are not everyday events, people tend to forget their power. Scientists, however, are working to develop new ways of detecting tsunamis so that better warning systems can be created.

Name________________________________

Use the passage on page 22 to complete the activities.
Write **S** next to the sentences that contain similes. Write **X** next to the sentences that do not contain similes.

1. ________ The village lay in a heap.
2. ________ It looked like a giant had come and pounded the houses flat.
3. ________ Tsunamis have stormed like angry monsters in many places around the globe.
4. ________ Large volumes of water are displaced and form into columns of water.
5. ________ When a tsunami reaches shallow water, like a harbor, it can build to an enormous height.
6. ________ Some of these waves look like four-story buildings.
7. ________ An underwater landslide is hidden, like a secret.
8. ________ The loose sediment cascades down like an avalanche.
9. ________ They felt the deck shake and saw a rock avalanche shower down from a mountain.
10. ________ The rocks roared into the bay like a herd of buffalo.
11. Write a three-sentence summary of "Walls of Water." Include at least one simile in your summary.

____

____

____

____

____

____

____

____

____

Read the passage. Then, answer the questions.

After the Storm

Returning back to my village and seeing the devastation of my hometown, it all seemed surreal. Since visiting my relatives and having such a great time, I had hardly missed home. Now back here, seeing the damage caused by the raging tsunami, I feel a twinge of guilt for feeling so relieved about not being here. The tsunami hit my village, killing thousands of innocent people. These natural occurrences don't seem to care who they harm. I am so angry with this treacherous mess! I am full of fury at this raging storm. I knew tsunamis were a dangerous force, but I had never seen anything like this. My village was swarming in despair and there's nothing we could have done to prevent it.

Survivors told me the waves were loud and looming. They were fast and as tall as four-story buildings. No one had time to prepare and many people were harmed. Many of my neighbors lost their homes and animals, some even lost their lives. Standing here today, I am grateful that I am safe, but sad at what is left of my land. We will rebuild, we will join together as a community and rebuild one home at a time. Even though disaster has embraced my village, we will survive with love. Devastation will not destroy our strength and perseverance.

1. What is the problem the narrator faces?

   ____

2. How does the narrator feel toward tsunamis? How do you know?

   ____

3. Why does the narrator feel guilty?

   ____

4. Compare and contrast "Walls of Water" on page 22 and "After the Storm." How does each author present information about the tsunamis? How are the passages similar? How are they different?

   ____

   ____

   ____

5. Research a natural disaster of your choice. What information do you learn? On a separate sheet of paper, write a short summary of your findings.

   ____

Name_______________________________

Read the passage. Then, answer the questions. Highlight evidence from the text to support your answers.

Mind Your (Animal) Manners

Even chimps learn manners. In one group, chimps stamp their feet to get attention. If they join a second group, they might be frowned at for that behavior. In the second group, chimps might knock their knuckles together to get attention.

Most people think of culture as the art, music, or literature of a group of people. Culture includes more. It includes behaviors and ways of life. Those behaviors can differ from society to society. Scientists are discovering that animals have culture, too, and that members of an animal group often teach others their culture. For example, one researcher taught primates to wash food before eating. When the females had babies, they passed this new behavior on to their infants, rearing a new generation of food-washers.

Even in the wild, culture exists. After a fight, female chimps hold grudges, but older males teach younger ones postures and gestures that show that they are ready to make peace. Many of us need to learn those kinds of manners!

1. What is the main idea of this passage?_______________________________

____

2. Did scientists always know that animals had culture?_______________________________

   What statement from the text supports your conclusion?

____

____

3. Does the author conclude that animals learn their culture or that animals inherit their culture? _______________________________

4. What conclusion can you draw about the purpose of culture in animals?

____

   What evidence from the text helped you to draw your conclusion?

____

____

____

Name________________________________

Summarizing

Read the passage. Then, answer the questions on page 27.

Mathew Brady's Career

Mathew Brady tried to end warfare for all time. He used a new, powerful weapon. He used a camera.

Brady opened his first photography studio in 1844. The images he produced were daguerreotypes, not the photographs he would take later. Daguerreotypes recorded images on sheets of copper coated with silver. They required long exposures, so the person being photographed would have to stay perfectly still for 3–15 minutes. That made daguerreotypes impractical for portraits. By 1855, Brady was advertising a new type of image that had just been invented: a photograph made on paper.

From the beginning of his career, Brady believed that photography could serve an important purpose. His images could create a record of national life. When the Civil War broke out, he wanted to document the war as a part of that record. His friends discouraged him, but Brady started to take photographs of war scenes. He assembled a corps of photographers who worked in the field, taking photographs of battle scenes and military life. He also bought photographs from others who were returning from the field. His efforts culminated in an 1862 display of photographs made after the Battle of Antietam. The bloodshed shocked the visitors to the exhibit, most of whom had never seen a field of battle.

Brady did not stop warfare with his work, but he did raise the awareness of the costs of war among common citizens. After the Civil War, people lost interest in his chronicle of the war. Because he could find few buyers for his photographs and did not earn enough money to pay for his wartime work, Brady went bankrupt. Years after the war, Congress bought Brady's collection. It is now considered a priceless documentation of the War between the States. Other photographs by Mathew Brady sell for thousands of dollars and are considered national treasures.

Name________________________________

Summarizing

Use the passage on page 26 to answer the questions.

1. Which sentence best summarizes this entire story?

   A. Mathew Brady went bankrupt, but now his photographs are valuable.

   B. Mathew Brady wanted to use photography to create a record of national life.

   C. Mathew Brady first took daguerreotypes, but switched to photographs.

   D. Mathew Brady was the first photographer in the United States.

2. Which sentence best summarizes the final paragraph of the story?

   A. Mathew Brady went bankrupt, but now his photographs are considered valuable.

   B. Mathew Brady helped to stop warfare in the United States.

   C. Mathew Brady's photographs of the Civil War were bought by Congress.

   D. Mathew Brady's work is not treasured today.

3. How did Mathew Brady chronicle the Civil War?

   A. He took photographs of wartime scenes.

   B. He assembled a group of photographers to take pictures of the war.

   C. He bought pictures from other photographers who were returning from the field.

   D. All of the above

4. Which sentence summarizes Brady's wartime efforts?

   A. His work shocked people so much that they did not want to see him.

   B. His work shocked people but raised their awareness of the costs of war.

   C. His work shocked most people but not members of Congress.

   D. His work is not considered valuable today.

5. Why do you think people were so shocked by Brady's photographs?

____

____

____

____

Name________________________________

Read the passage. Then, complete the activities on page 29.

The Irish Famine

On May 1, 1848, the *Swan* set sail from Cork, Ireland. The ship carried victims of the Irish famine to a new life in North America.

The passengers watched as Ireland disappeared on the horizon behind them. They were leaving their home forever. But they were also leaving the horrors of the past few years. Fields lay black with rot, and relatives died of starvation and disease. Their trials were not over when they boarded the ship, however. Ahead stretched a dangerous voyage. On ships transporting these Irish citizens, cholera and other diseases passed from one person to the next, infecting everyone and often killing up to one-third of the passengers. The newspapers of the time called the emigration ships "coffin ships" because of the high death rate aboard them.

It was a single crop that started the problem, a crop on which the poor of Ireland were too dependent: the potato. Through generations, Irish parents and their grown children divided farms into smaller and smaller lots. Grain could not be grown on these small plots of land, but potatoes could. Poor Irish families depended almost entirely on this plant for food, and grew the same varieties year after year. When the plant virus known as the potato blight was accidentally introduced into the country in 1845, it spread quickly throughout the country. Year after year, the crops died. So did the Irish people. So many people died that relatives could not buy coffins, even if they had the money to do so. Entire families and whole villages were wiped out. It was the worst European famine of the 19th century.

The famine changed Ireland in many ways. After the famine ended, farmers tried new methods and new crops to avoid the tragedy of the past. The Irish people varied their diet. They mourned the people they had lost through death and emigration to North America. In 1844, Ireland's population was over eight million people. By 1851, more than a million were dead, and a million and a half more had emigrated to North America. The lowly potato had changed a country and its people forever.

Name______________________________

Use the passage on page 28 to to complete the activities.

Match the two parts of each sentence. Then, use this information to write a summary of the passage.

1.	________ The Irish Famine occurred	A.	wiped out from starvation.
2.	________ The crops of the Irish people	B.	between 1845 and 1851.
3.	________ Whole villages were	C.	of the 19th century.
4.	________ It was the worst European famine	D.	was reduced by two and a half million.
5.	________ By the end of the famine, the population of Ireland	E.	were killed by potato blight.
6.	________ After the famine,	F.	farmers varied their crops and methods.

7. Write a summary of the passage.

Name________________________________

Read the passage. Then, answer the questions on page 31.

A Journey of Hope

"Good-bye," I whisper to my neighbor and friend, Dominique. We hug each other and promise to always remember the times we shared in this once beautiful country. I have known and been friends with Dominique my entire life. She is the best friend in all of Ireland. I know that we will never see each other again, but at least she is alive. Dominique will not travel with me on my journey to America because her mother is too sick for the voyage and her family doesn't want to leave without her.

We lost grandmother to the famine. After her funeral, I was so grief-stricken, I cried for days, unable to understand how this could possibly be happening to my family. I don't want to leave Dominique, but I know my family will be safe when we arrive in America to live with my uncle. He is eagerly waiting for us. Health and peace are waiting as well; at least that's what my mother says.

The day I found out we had to leave, I yelled and screamed in protest, "This disgusting, hateful famine has taken everything from me! I won't go and leave my friends, and leave my home!"

Mother sat beside me, rubbing my hair and wiping my tears. "It has been a terrible time for us," she started, "but if we make it to America, we will be safe." I knew what she meant by "if we make it." I had heard terrible stories about the ships that would take us to America. The conditions were frightening. Many diseases were spread and many people died. I was afraid and angry. My mother read my face.

"We will be fine," she told me. "I believe that we will, I know we will." I wondered if her words were to comfort me, or to comfort her. As the tears streamed down her face, I knew she was troubled and **apprehensive**. The past few years had been horrendous. Our main source of food had been potatoes. Once the potato blight came, it destroyed all of our crops, and many of my family's friends died. It was not until we lost grandmother that my family realized the terrible shape we were in. My mother worried that we would not survive here. We had very little food to eat and we were all getting weak. My father made the decision to travel to America. Looking at my mother, it was clear that even though she was afraid of what might happen on the ship, she believed that what could happen to us here was worse. I didn't want to be selfish and make the situation more difficult.

"You are right, mother, we will go to America. We will be safe there; we will build a new life. I will make new friends and always hold on to the memory of grandmother and Dominique." I smiled, hoping to convince my mother that I was okay. Gazing into her eyes, I knew I had to believe that she and my father were right, health and peace would be waiting for us.

And hope, hope would be there in America as well. We would build a new life and forever remember our native country. I packed my things for our journey, knowing in my heart we would be safe. We would travel to America and begin again.

Name______________________________

Use the passages on pages 28 and 30 to answer the questions.

1. At what point did the narrator's family decide they should leave?

2. How does the potato blight impact the narrator's life?

3. At the beginning of the story, how does the narrator feel about leaving? What happens to make her change her mind?

4. What can you infer about the narrator? Cite evidence from the text to support your answer.

5. What does *apprehensive* mean?

6. Why might the narrator's mother be apprehensive?

7. Compare and contrast "The Irish Famine" on page 28 to "A Journey of Hope." How does each author present information about the famine? How are the passages similar? How are they different?

8. On a separate sheet of paper, write a summary of the passage.

Name____

Compare/Contrast

Read the passage. Then, complete the activities on page 33.

Canoes

Canoes have been around for hundreds of years and have been made in all shapes and sizes. Generally, a canoe is thought of as a boat that is pointed at both ends with a relatively flat bottom. It is wider in the middle than at the ends. This makes it buoyant enough to be used in shallow water and stable enough to be used in deep water. Canoes are usually propelled by paddles, but some can also be sailed.

The name canoe comes from the Spanish version of an Arawak word, *canao*. The Arawaks were people who lived on islands in the Caribbean. They made their canoes, known as **dugouts**, from whole pieces of trees. They chose a tree that was the right length for a canoe, cut it down, trimmed off all the branches, and hauled it close to the water's edge. While removing the bark, they scraped an outline of the area they would hollow out to create the interior of the canoe. Then they dumped hot coals on this outlined spot to burn out a cockpit. Dippers of water were used to control the fire. The burning also dried the sap from the log, making the boat waterproof. Then the Arawaks carved the ends into points to help the boat glide through the water. This dugout would be paddled by two people, both of whom steered.

A **kayak** is another form of a canoe. The kayak was developed by the Inuits—natives of Greenland, the Arctic Circle, and the Hudson Bay coastline of North America. These natives made kayaks by constructing frames of driftwood or animal bones, which they bound together with gut. The frame was covered completely in sealskin, except for a hole at the top that created the cockpit. The sealskin, which was sewn onto the frame, was naturally waterproof. A kayak is paddled by only one person, who has to steer by him- or herself.

Canoes have served as basic water transportation for people of many cultures. The canoe that is most familiar to us today was a design perfected by American Indians. Today, the canoe is used mainly for recreation. It allows its paddlers to explore waterways that cannot be reached by other means. It's easy to haul a canoe onto shore when it's time to camp for the night. Its stability and ease of use make it a great vehicle for a short or long trip.

Name________________________________

Compare/Contrast

Use the passage on page 32 to complete the activities.

1. Explain why the canoe can be used in shallow and deep water. Use evidence from the text to support your answer.

____

____

2. In your own words, write a summary of how the Arawaks made canoes.

____

____

____

3. Use the Venn diagram to compare and contrast the dugout and the kayak. Use evidence from the text.

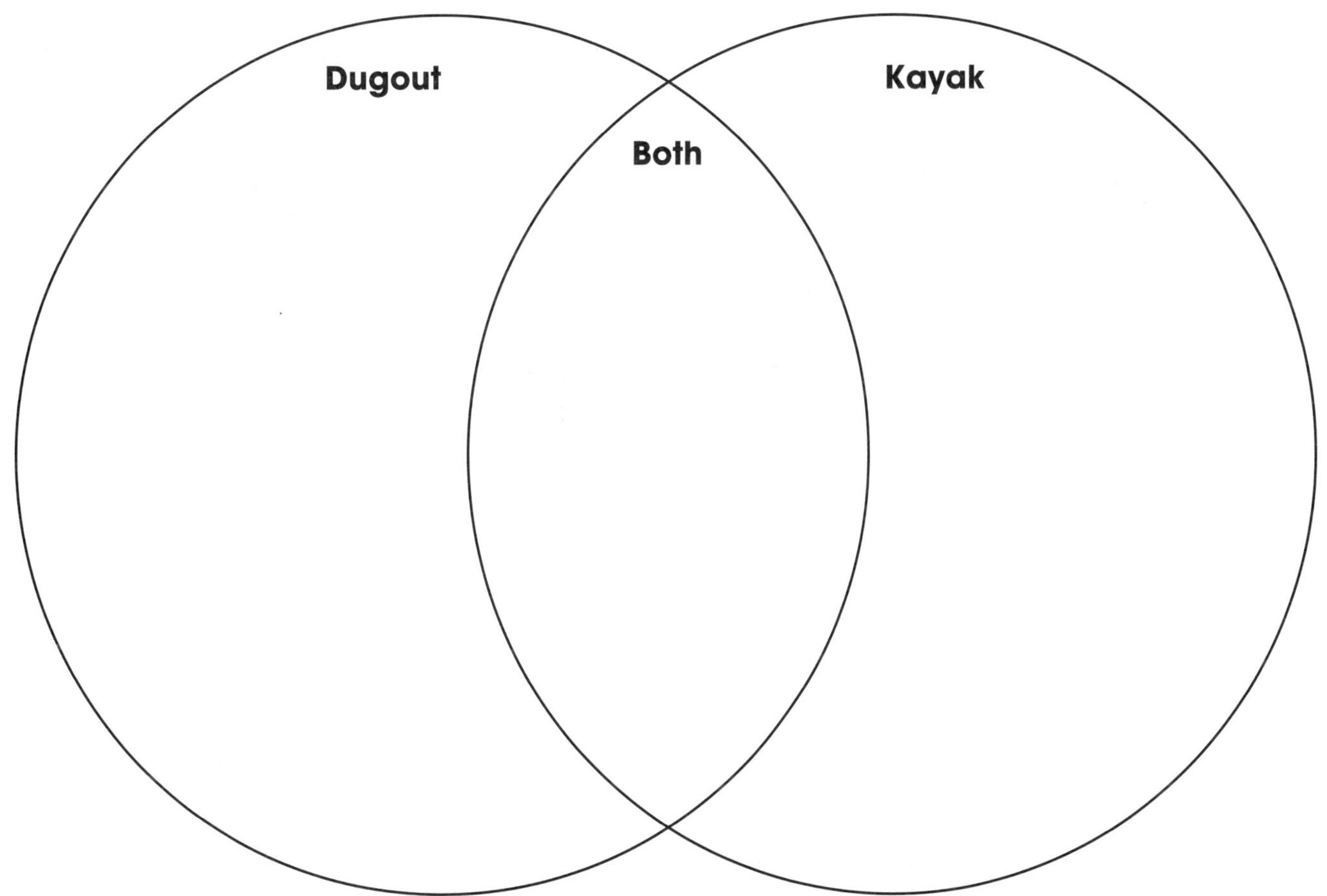

Name________________________________

Read the passage. Then, answer the questions on page 35.

At Shauna's House

"I'm starving," said Kelly as she and Shauna walked home from school.

Shauna sighed. "You're always starving," she said. "We'll have something when we get to my house."

Kelly looked at Shauna, who was walking quickly down the sidewalk. Shauna had long, beautiful red hair and always wore perfect outfits. Kelly had short hair and many of her clothes were hand-me-downs.

No one was home when they got to Shauna's house. No one ever seemed to be home at Shauna's house. Kelly had two sisters and a brother. "It must be amazing to have the whole house to yourself. I'm lucky if I can be alone for five minutes," said Kelly.

"It's awesome," Shauna replied. "I can do whatever I want. Do you want to order a pizza? There's nothing in the refrigerator." There was never anything in Shauna's refrigerator.

"That's okay," said Kelly. "I have to go home for dinner soon."

Shauna rolled her eyes. "I would go crazy if people were telling me what to do all the time."

"Well, you're lucky," said Kelly. Shauna was lucky. She had perfect hair, perfect clothes, a perfect house. "I would give anything to be Shauna for just one day," thought Kelly.

The phone rang. "Hi, Mom," Kelly heard Shauna say. "No, it's okay. I understand." She hung up. "My mom's having dinner out again," she said. "Are you sure you can't stay for pizza?"

"Sorry. I have to go or I'll be late for dinner," said Kelly.

"Whatever. See you."

Kelly saw Shauna looking out the window as she walked down the street. Suddenly, Shauna's house looked very big, and Shauna looked very small.

Name________________________________

Use the passage on page 34 to answer the questions.

1. Which of these is the best contrast between Shauna's life and Kelly's?

   A. Shauna is from a big family and Kelly is from a small one.

   B. Kelly has a big, caring family and Shauna is often on her own.

   C. Kelly has perfect clothes and Shauna wears hand-me-downs.

   D. Shauna and Kelly have similar family situations.

2. Which of these contrasts is true?

   A. Kelly has brothers and sisters; Shauna is an only child.

   B. Shauna's mother does not have much money; Kelly's parents are wealthy.

   C. Kelly is a good student; Shauna is a struggling student.

   D. Kelly lives in a big house; Shauna lives in a smaller house.

3. Which things about Shauna's life does Kelly envy?

   A. her house, her parents, and her clothes

   B. her hair, her clothes, and her pets

   C. her hair, her clothes, and her house

   D. her clothes, her parents, and her pets

4. What things about Kelly's life might Shauna envy?

   A. the fact that Kelly has sisters to loan her clothes

   B. the fact that Kelly has caring parents who are there to take care of her

   C. the fact that Kelly has a big house and lots of time to herself

   D. the fact that Kelly gets to eat pizza almost every night of the week

5. How does Kelly's perspective of Shauna change by the end of the text? How does the author let you know this?

____

____

____

____

____

____

Read the reports. Then, complete the activities on page 37.

Hello, and Good Evening

During Choose a Profession Week, Fiona Foster bummed around with her uncle, Blake Becker, the local television personality. For three days she wrote and reported on-the-air on three different topics.

(1) You think it's hot now! Well, I'm telling you it's going to be a downright scorcher the next couple of days. According to Emmett King, our chief regional meteorologist, cool relief won't be in sight until the middle of next week. Bring out the fans and air conditioners. Nighttime temperatures are expected to drop only to the mid 80s. Today was the fourth day of 100 degree heat. And the rain promised earlier today? Oops! Put those umbrellas away. This reporter was reading off the wrong chart. That's it for the weather. Back to you, Uncle Blake.

(2) Funeral services will be held tomorrow, the twenty-second, for Hannah Daniels, a longtime member of the local Humane Society. Many of us have fond memories of Hannah, who was a friend to creatures. When a vicious chickadee recently cornered George Johnson's adorable, harmless cobra, it was Hannah who scared the fearsome bird away. Her sensitive care for the less fortunate was always readily apparent. Her nephew, Byron, remembers how she reacted when her puppies were frightened by a neighbor's wandering tabby. "Why, Aunt Hannah, she done took that feline by the tail and flung her into a wild raspberry patch," he recalls. On Saturday, Ms. Daniels passed away peacefully while resting in her rocking chair. In lieu of flowers, family members ask that donations be made to the Dog-B-Good Biscuit Company.

(3) Once again Paige Palmer slams her Wabash Wildcats to victory with a two-out, bases-loaded, three-bagger in the ninth inning of their contest against the neighboring Bridgeport Bunions. The 5′ 10″, first-base all-star scored twice and hit safely four times in this heavy-handed slugfest that concluded with the score of 11–9. The Bunions' assistant coach remarked, "With her power, Palmer can play pro ball anytime." Tia Throwhart pitched the Wildcats to victory. Sally Southpaugh suffered the heart-breaking loss.

Name____________________

Use the reports on page 36 to complete the activities. Highlight evidence from the text to support your answers.

1. How would you describe these five people?

   Hannah Daniels ____________________

   Emmett King ____________________

   Sally Southpaugh ____________________

   George Johnson ____________________

   Paige Palmer ____________________

2. Circle the central ideas of Fiona's three television reports.

   Report 1

   weather sports national news advertising death

   Report 2

   weather sports national news advertising death

   Report 3

   weather sports national news advertising death

3. Write a word from each report to match the definition of the words below.

   Report 1

   extremely hot day ____________________

   weather scientist ____________________

   Report 2

   feline ____________________

   tender ____________________

   Report 3

   three times ____________________

   competition, game ____________________

Name_______________________________

Read the passage. Then, answer the questions on page 39.

American Graffiti

Stuck in front of the tube again. Just stuck.

No energy to stop being lazy and go play ball. No will to get up and do his house chores. Not even enough **gumption** to raid the fridge for a snack.

Not that the TV had much to offer.

There was that stupid soap about all these lovelorn grownups acting like...well, actually acting younger than he felt. There was that weird courtroom drama where adults yelled and screamed at each other as though they were really angry. Like it was the end of the world or something. As if we really cared.

He blipped to another station. Oh, yeah, a game show. The host had a slicked-back pompadour. His sidekick was a blond whose thick mane swished back and forth whenever she knew the camera was pointing her way.

Futility. Wasted time.

He punched the remote again.

"...And now this tragic news from Beijing. Twenty million are believed to be dead following the worst natural disaster in written history. A tsunami, whose wave heights reached upwards of one hundred feet, roared up from the southeast, slamming into the port cities of Macau, Shantow, and the former English enclave of Hong Kong. China's government officials, world relief agencies, and United Nations delegates are scrambling to assess the damage and to begin rescue and relief efforts...."

He dropped the remote and stared intently at the screen.

Whoa! This was bad! Since fifth grade when he'd first read and researched the nation of China, he had been fascinated by any news pertaining to that country.

"...The following scenes may be too graphic and disturbing for some of our viewers. **Parental discretion** is advised..."

The camera zoomed in on the destruction of buildings, of forests and fields, of animals, and of human life. Muddy rivers of water and debris pulled back to the sea. The water washed away much of the landscape's former beauty and left a desolate scene of mud, decay, and despair. Trees had snapped off. Roofs were wrapped around branches. An animal, perhaps an ox, bobbed up and down as the swirling current shoved it out of the camera's view.

The boy's hands shook. What a price these people had to pay! What awful, awesome power the earthquake under the ocean's floor had unleashed. But he could bear it no more. He had to escape the sights and sounds of this news broadcast.

He intended to push the power switch. He missed.

"I'd like to buy a vowel, Tripp," the twangy mid-western voice moaned.

Click.

"Don't your raise your voice in this court, young lady!"

"I was just..."

Click.

Name______________________________

Use the passage on page 38 to answer the questions. Highlight evidence from the text to support your answers.

1. What is the "tube"? ______________________________
2. Write a synonym for *gumption*. ______________________________
3. What do you think *parental discretion* means? ______________________________

   ____
4. Why does the narrator keep changing the television channel?

   ____

   ____
5. What was the one thing that interested the narrator on the television? Why?

   ____

   ____
6. Why does the narrator change the channel from the program that interests him the most? ______________________________

   ____

   ____
7. What can you infer about the narrator? ______________________________

   ____

   ____

Name____________________

Read the passage. Then, answer the questions. Highlight evidence from the text to support your answers.

Television Time

People have long discussed the benefits and drawbacks of TV time. Researchers say children begin watching TV at a very young age. Some toddlers watch 2 hours a day. Some school age children spend about 4 hours a day watching television.

Some people say that TV can be good because it gives students an opportunity to learn through educational programming. Students can learn about real world events through news outlets on TV or watch shows about science and nature. However, TV can also take away time students spend exercising or spending time with family or friends.

Too much TV has been linked to obesity. People can spend hours sitting in front of the television and not get any exercise. In addition, some TV programs show violence and behaviors that are not appropriate for children. Some people think children should not be allowed to watch TV at all. Some people think there should be more educational TV shows for children. However, most people will agree, regardless of how much time is spent watching television, parents should monitor what their children view on the screen.

1. How much time do children spend watching television?

 ____

2. What is the author's purpose for writing this passage?

 ____

3. What are some benefits of watching television?

 ____

4. What are some drawbacks of watching television?

 ____

5. Compare and contrast "American Graffiti" on page 38 and "Television Time." How does each author present information about too much TV? How are the passages similar? How are they different?

 ____

 ____

 ____

Name___________________________________

Conduct a survey that asks your classmates how much television they watch. Interview at least 10 classmates. Use the chart to record how much television students in your class watch. What are their favorite shows? What are their opinions about television? Do they see it as good or bad? Why? Do they think they watch too much television? Write a brief summary that explains your findings. Is what you learned in the passage "Television Time" consistent with your classmates' responses?

Name	How much TV do you watch?	Do you think you watch too much TV?	Is TV good or bad? Why?
1.			
2.			
3.			
4.			
5.			
6.			
7.			
8.			
9.			
10.			

Summary of findings:

____

____

____

____

____

____

____

____

Name________________________________

Citing Textual Evidence

Read the passage. Then, answer the questions on page 43.

Guilt

He stumbled off to his bedroom, found a sheet of paper, and grabbed his Valentine's Day pencil. He plunked down on the hardwood floor under his bed to write.

Dear Mama,

I love you but I am sorry. I broked your favrit dish. You know the one Daddy got you and you cried and said YOU just loved it. Well I broked it.

I didn't try to. Really. I was juest playing with Spud and we was chasin aroud the table and I knock into the table and the dish felt off and broked.

I love you Mama.

And I know that you must hate me. And I am sorry. I will go away and I won't bother you agin and maybe you and Daddy can fix the dish with some glue. I tried the white glue but it didn't work too good.

Maybe if you fix the dish you will want me back. I hope so cuz I miss you already and I'm not even gone yet and I love you so and...

He began to cry. Softly. Whimpering like a cocker puppy with tears rolling down his cheeks like raindrops on a windowpane in a summer downpour. Quietly, so as not to draw attention. Muffled, to hold all his pain to himself. The young boy slept.

He woke to hear Mama coming in from the garden, walking to the kitchen to wash her hands. The child quickly scrawled his hugs and kisses, signed his name Brady, placed his missive on the teddy bear comforter of his bed, and stepped into his closet. He'd have to leave when the house was quiet, he thought. Maybe midnight. Yeah, it'd be dark then.

So the boy waited and waited. And he had to go to the bathroom because waiting was so hard, but he didn't want Mama to see him. So he sat down on the floor in his closet and quietly cried himself to sleep again.

Mama found the shards of glass. Mama found the glue bottle tipped over, still dripping thick, glossy beads to the floor. She guessed. She sighed.

Mama traced the boy's route to his room. To his bed. To his note, which she could hardly read through her own tears. And to the closet where, scooping up her seven-year-old son, she held him like a newborn, cradled in her arms, feeling his tousled, tear-stained head below her cheek. She pulled him to her and carried him to her favorite rocker. And she held him tight, held him long past the time he'd wake up and say,

"Oh, Mama, I love you!"

And they'd cry again.

Name________________________________

Use the passage on page 42 to answer the questions. Highlight evidence from the text to support your answers.

1. What is the boy's crime?

____

2. What is compared to raindrops? Why do you think the author makes this comparison?

____

____

3. The author gives two reasons why the boy cries quietly. What are they?

____

____

4. What do you believe Mama's feelings are when she discovers the glass shards?

____

____

5. How does Mama react when she finds Brady?

____

____

6. What words in the story are synonyms for the following:

   a. note/message ______________________________

   b. quilt/blanket ______________________________

   c. dropped/thudded ______________________________

Name________________________________

Read the passage. Then answer the questions on page 45.

A Moral Dilemma

A couple of years ago, Wesley Hamilton and his family lived in Central America. Both of his parents taught in an English-speaking school there, and Wesley was able to learn Spanish with the aid of eager classmates. Wes enjoyed living in new surroundings. He met new people and made new friends. He appreciated the world experience.

But Wesley was troubled much of the time. This Latin American country was so poor! In the large city below his home lived some wealthy families. They had large, well-groomed mansions, walled homes, and many great luxuries. There also lived many poor people in their simple homes. Some were mud and brick, some wooden slabs, some cardboard or corrugated metal. Many homes had dirt floors and no electricity. The children of these homes might have jobs of walking to the community well to haul water back to their houses. The rich had servants, gardens, cars, clothing, plenty. The poor had...well, what did they have?

A few months earlier, before Wesley and his family went to this land, they took classes called "orientation workshops." They were told what to expect in this country. There were many beggars. Their trainer warned them not to give them money. It keeps them begging, he explained. Begging doesn't teach people how to be constructive members of society. And parents may force kids to beg. That's wrong, he said.

Maybe so. But Wesley became very uncomfortable seeing such poverty. There was a little girl in a blue dress who sold flowers with her blind grandmother. The girl, maybe seven or eight years old, took care of all the money from their sales. She always smiled. But she had such big, dark eyes. And she looked kind of frail.

The worst feeling Wesley Hamilton experienced happened when he ate at restaurants. You see, the poor people couldn't afford to eat at such places but the rich people ate out all the time. One day a young woman with two babies, one still an infant, begged for food as the Hamiltons left a restaurant. Wesley's mom gave her a chicken leg and a cup of mashed potatoes. Another time, Wesley was seated out on a restaurant patio, chowing down on a hamburger when he heard a whispered plea. Two dirty hands stretched out through some foliage and a small boy's voice called, "Please, please!" A store manager heard the pleas and sternly ordered the child to leave.

Wesley didn't understand. Why were North Americans so rich? Do we deserve to be better off than others? What could he do for the people that were hungry? Why was life so unfair?

Wesley sat at his desk daydreaming. He was wearing a sweater and jeans. He had on a pair of name-brand shoes. He turned to see his class computer station. The room hummed as the air control unit blew out a steady stream of comfortable and comforting warm air. His stomach growled, telling him that it was about time to eat. He imagined he would eat only half the food he got at lunch. He would probably throw away the rest.

But, that was all right in the United States. Or was it?

Name________________________________

Use the passage on page 44 to answer the questions. Highlight evidence from the text to support your answers.

1. What character traits would you use to describe Wesley?

____

____

2. What is Wesley's main concern?

____

____

____

3. According to Wesley's instructor, why should people not give beggars money? Does Wesley agree?

____

____

____

4. Why does Wesley think Americans are wasteful?

____

____

____

5. How does Wesley's setting impact how he feels about his life in America?

____

____

____

Name____________________________________

Read the passage. Then, answer the questions on page 47.

How'd You Like That?

Here's food for thought. Today in most world communities, if you are hungry for meat, you go to a restaurant or a food market, pick up your beef, pork, mutton, fowl, or fish, and simply return home. Even families who enjoy hunting buy their own meat. Of course that wasn't always so.

In times and places where agriculture was unknown or unavailable, humans had to hunt to survive. One such people were the American Indians of the Great American Plains. These well-practiced hunters consumed antelope, rabbit, fish, and quail, but their primary resource was bison. The trick was knowing how to hunt the beast.

These hunters used their spears and javelins to hunt the bison. They utilized the bow, too. But hunting bison is no easy walk through the park. Remember, bison are large creatures and could travel with speed, and the hunters, horseless before Coronado's travels, were hard pressed to keep up. The stubborn and ornery adult bison was no easy prey for the unskilled hunter.

Imagine a young hunter who has trekked 20 or more miles unaccompanied across the grassy plains in search of his first bison. He walks and walks until finally, climbing over a grassy knoll, he sees before him a herd of a hundred thousand bison. His sudden appearance startles them. A few adult bison turn to stare briefly before instigating the thunderous stampede, which in minutes leaves the hunter alone once more. Can you imagine the gibes of his people when he returns to his village? Or their bitter disappointment in hunger?

We know that hunters of these plains sometimes wore skins of animals to cover their scent and hide their human features. The hides of a coyote or a wolf could be draped over one's body. Though these canines were no friend of the bison, their presence would be of little alarm to the adult herd, who knew well how to protect their young. So poised for the hunt, fur-covered hunters could creep within range of the bison undiscovered.

In another remarkable method of hunting bison, hunters searching for bison near rivers sometimes used cliffs and bluffs into which river water had cut deep grooves. If these hunters were fortunate to find bison herds nearby, they formed a human corral of people with hunters forming the two side "fences." A noisy, boisterous lot of hunters would startle the beasts and drive them forward, and the bison, attempting to avoid the human wall of hunters, would pass between the two fences. Those hunters on the wall had a most dangerous duty. They had to hold their ground despite the anguishing bellow of bison desperately seeking to escape. If all went as planned, bison would rush toward the cliff's edge. Some would finally escape thorough the fences of hunters who had already obtained all the bison they would need for their families.

After this, hunters could use the bison for food, clothing, shelters, and tools. This process is very different from going to the store to get what you need, as many of us do today.

Name________________________________

Use the passage on page 46 to answer the questions. Highlight evidence from the text to support your answers.

1. Who is this passage about?

____

____

2. What was their chief source of food?

____

3. What was the difficulty of killing the animal?

____

____

4. How might the hunters camouflage themselves?

____

____

5. What formed the fences described here?

____

____

6. How did hunting change with the arrival of the Europeans?

____

____

7. Write a word from the passage that is a synonym for *noisy* or *raucous*.

____

8. Write a word from the passage that is a synonym for *crevices*.

____

9. Write a word from the passage that is a homophone for *sent*.

____

Name_______________________________

Read the passage. Then, answer the questions. Highlight evidence from the text to support your answers.

In Your Face

Patsy Pappas begged her parents for permission to explore the new In Your Face Zoo in Bistro, Sri Lanka. The zoo is divided into three pods, named Reptile Row, Matrix of Mammals, and Bird Boutique.

Although she desired a larger selection of critters and found the pod names ridiculous, Patsy loved the opportunity to get this close to the animals. In all cases but one, she touched the creatures. So much for wild!

In the Matrix of Mammals, Patsy stroked two members of the cat family, the Siberian tiger and the jaguar. The lynx, in a foul mood, kept its distance. One of the bears of the Kodiak, who had just taken an icy dip, had cold, smelly, and wet fur. However, the panda and polar bear, Patsy discovered, had very soft fur.

Reptiles are Patsy's joy. A python curled around her neck, and she fed the glass snake and coral snake with the attendant's assistance. Of the lizards, she found the gila monster most personable. Neither the monitor nor gecko gave her much notice, barely acknowledging her presence. So she left the Row in a huff.

At the Bird Boutique Patsy swam with the wood duck, hid with the ruffed grouse, and chortled with the wild turkey. No wonder they're called "game" birds! The golden eagle and osprey were eating during her visit, which was cool. The barred owl, also a predator, sat on Patsy's shoulder and nipped pleasantly at her ear. What a day!

1. How did Patsy interact with the animals?

____

____

2. What animal did Patsy decide not to pet? Why?

____

____

3. What is the central idea of the text? How does the author develop this idea throughout the text?

____

____

4. Choose one of the animals Patsy interacts with. Research information about the animal. On a separate sheet of paper, write a summary of your findings.

Name________________________

Read the schedule. Then, answer the questions. Highlight evidence from the text to support your answers.

Spinnin' Wheels

Thad Taylor, the top-seeded cyclist for the Pan American squad, has a busy morning schedule. After all, he is a student, an athlete, and a celebrity.

6:30	Walk Hercules
6:50	Bring Hercules to the petsitter
7:00	Breakfast with champions at the All-Flakes Bowl Inn
7:30	Take taxi to arena; change clothes in private suite
7:50	Stretching exercises
8:00	Private bike practice with Lee Schwinn
9:00	Tape interview with Chrissie Foster from the *Yesterday Show*
9:45	Take taxi to university; have power snack (granola bar)
10:00	Private instruction for Anthropology 312 (bring toothbrush)
11:00	Meet with study group at University Library. Topic: caterpillar diseases
12:20	Call agent

1. Who interviews Thad? ________________________

2. What is Thad's power snack? ________________________

3. What is the total amount of time Thad is scheduled to spend on his studies?

____

4. Who is Hercules? ________________________

5. What will Thad's study group discuss? ________________________

6. Where is breakfast? ________________________

7. How much time is scheduled for the interview? ________________________

8. Where must Thad bring his toothbrush? ________________________

9. How much time is spent on stretching exercises? ________________________

10. If Thad speaks with his agent for 17 minutes, what time is it when he gets off the phone?

____

Name____________________________

Read the contract. Then, answer the questions. Highlight evidence from the text to support your answers.

A Contractual Agreement

The owners of *Sports Freaks* at 1968 Lolich Lane do hearby agree to hire *Green Thumb Lawncare Services* and pay them for services rendered under the conditions that follow.

Green Thumb Lawncare Services agrees to:

A
1. Mow weekly beginning the third full week of April and continue for 24 weeks through the first week of October.
2. Edge all business driveways and sidewalks monthly.
3. Trim grass from around trees, bushes, signs, and statues.
4. Remove or blow all loose grass clippings from driveways and walkways.
5. Provide aforementioned lawn care either on Monday or Tuesday of each week between the hours of 8:30 am and 5:30 pm.

In return *Sports Freaks* agrees to:

B
1. Make payments in timely, monthly order by the fifteenth of each month beginning May 15 for a total of six payments for $200 each.
2. Keep gates open and the grounds accessible for the ground crews to work. Any additional work (bush trimming or fall leaf collection, for example) will be handled under a separate contract.

Signatures: Michael Martinze
President, *Sports Freaks*
Perry Walsh
Treasurer, *Green Thumb Lawncare Services*

1. What is the address of the business to be cared for?________________
2. How many payments will be made?________________
3. Who is Michael Martinez?________________
4. Does the lawn service have to trim bushes?________________
5. Why must *Sports Freaks* agree to B2?________________
6. What is the total payment by *Sports Freaks* for services rendered?________________
7. Who signed this contract on *Green Thumb's* behalf?________________
8. How many weeks will the service work?________________
9. On what days of the week must *Green Thumb* do its work?________________

Name________________________________

Read the title of the page and the first paragraph of the passage below. Decide what main idea the article will discuss. Then, scan the article quickly for specific details that will help support that main idea. Highlight those details.

Dreaming Up a Good Grade

You've got a big test tomorrow. You decide to stay up all night studying, but that's a big mistake. If you're going to do your best on that test, you need to dream about it.

Two studies indicate that dreams help you sort out and remember new information or tasks. During a study in Belgium, volunteers watched symbols flash across a screen. The test required them to press the same symbol on a keyboard. Some volunteers worked on the test for several hours, slept, and then retook the test upon waking. They improved their scores. During the tests, scans of their brains highlighted the most active areas. Those same areas appeared most active during their dreams. Researchers believe that the volunteers practiced the test in their dreams and then stored what they learned.

A study by Dr. Robert Stickgold, a psychiatrist at Harvard Medical School, showed the same result. Volunteers played a computer game. Two thirds of those volunteers dreamed about the game. Stickgold concluded that dreams help people sort out new experiences and store them in long-term memory. His research included volunteers with damage to the **hippocampus**, a part of the brain that remembers what happens in the past. The people with damage to the hippocampus could not store the memories sorted out during their dreams. Although dreams do not originate in the hippocampus, that part of the brain apparently played a part in storing the memories.

These two research studies confirm what your mother always told you: You need a good night's sleep if you want to do your best.

1. Summarize the results of the dream studies discussed in the article.

____

____

____

2. What is the role of the *hippocampus*?________________________

____

3. What is the name of the Harvard psychiatrist who conducted one of the studies?

____

4. What portion of volunteers in the Harvard study dreamed about the computer game?

____

Name____________________________________

Read the passage. Then, complete the activities on page 53.

Amber

Where can you find 100 million-year-old dinosaur blood? From amber, a substance known more for its decorative uses than for its scientific value—that is, until recently.

Amber is actually hardened tree resin that has been fossilized. Most of it is mined in the Baltic Sea area. It is smooth and warms quickly to the touch. Amber has been valued as a gemstone since prehistoric times. The ancient Greeks called it "electron," perhaps because amber builds up a small, negative charge when it is rubbed. The Romans thought that amber had medicinal properties. It also was used as a type of currency in ancient trade routes. Most often, amber is translucent red, yellow, orange, or gold—colors that were rare and valued. It was used for jewelry and for good-luck charms.

Perhaps the height of amber's decorative powers could be seen in a Russian palace. In the 1700s, an entire room of 100,000 carved and interlocking amber pieces was given as a gift to Tsar Peter the Great. This golden room, lit by more than 500 candles, was said to be dazzling in its beauty. However, the room is now missing. The Nazis stole the room during World War II, dismantling and hiding it. A replica is being made of the room from drawings and paintings, but the search continues for the original, which is now worth approximately $200 million.

Today, the focus on amber has changed from decorative to scientific. This gemstone helps scientists learn about life millions of years ago. One in every 100 pieces of amber currently mined in the Dominican Republic contains a plant, insect, or tiny animal from prehistoric times. The once-living matter fossilized in amber can tell us about animal and plant diversity, the ecology of the landscape, and even how living things interacted with each other. Because of discoveries captured in amber, scientists have had to revise some of their evolutionary theories.

An even bigger breakthrough has been the ability to isolate and identify DNA of insects found in amber. This ability may one day lead to the isolation of dinosaur DNA. How? If a fossilized insect bit a dinosaur, it may be carrying that DNA. The problem is being able to recognize dinosaur DNA from millions of other sequences.

From art to science, the amazing story of amber continues!

Name________________________________

Fact or Opinion

Use the passage on page 52 to complete the activities.
Read each statement. Write **F** if it is a fact or **O** if it is an opinion.

_____ 1. Amber is hardened tree resin that has been fossilized.

_____ 2. Because of amber, scientists have had to revise some theories about evolution.

_____ 3. DNA research is the most significant scientific breakthrough this planet has ever known.

_____ 4. Most amber is mined in the Baltic Sea area.

_____ 5. The amber room was the most beautiful work of architecture in the 1700s.

_____ 6. The amber room of Tsar Peter the Great is being recreated, but the original is missing.

_____ 7. The amber room of Tsar Peter the Great is worth approximately $200 million.

_____ 8. Many pieces of amber contain fossilized insects, plants, or animals.

_____ 9. The study of dinosaur DNA is very dangerous.

_____ 10. Amber could probably be used as medicine again, just as the Romans used it.

11. How can amber help scientists?

____

____

12. How has the focus on amber changed over the years? Use specific examples from the text to support your answer.

____

____

____

____

Name________________________________

Read the passage. Then, complete the activity on page 55.

The Tale of an Ancient Sailor

Professor Francesco Mallegni often thinks about the sailor who died clutching his dog. The sailor had raised his right arm. Perhaps he tried to shield himself and his dog from the shifting cargo. Rope had snarled his foot, probably when he returned to the hold to rescue the dog.

The sailor died more than 2,000 years ago near the harbor of Pisa, Italy. Thanks to Mallegni and his Italian research team, visitors to a traveling exhibit can look this ancient sailor in the eye. Mallegni and his team developed a computer program that scanned the sailor's skull. His team's computer program accounted for cultural and historical differences in the thicknesses of muscles and skin. Then the program reconstructed the sailor's face.

Already, Mallegni's team has reconstructed the faces of the ancient Roman sailor, a young Egyptian soldier, and an Egyptian prince. Recently, the team reconstructed the face of an ancient Roman man whom Mallegni believes to be the famous Italian painter Giotto. The reconstructed face looks like a painting that some think might be Giotto's self-portrait.

These ancient people fascinate Mallegni. The pattern of wear on the teeth of the artist's skull revealed that he had probably held his paintbrush between his teeth. The sailor's skull showed that he was about 40 when he died. The Egyptian soldier's skull revealed that he had probably died of a battle wound. Mallegni thinks that the sailor looks as if he could live in the house next door. Through Mallegni's fascination and attention to detail, these ancient people come alive for today's museum visitors too.

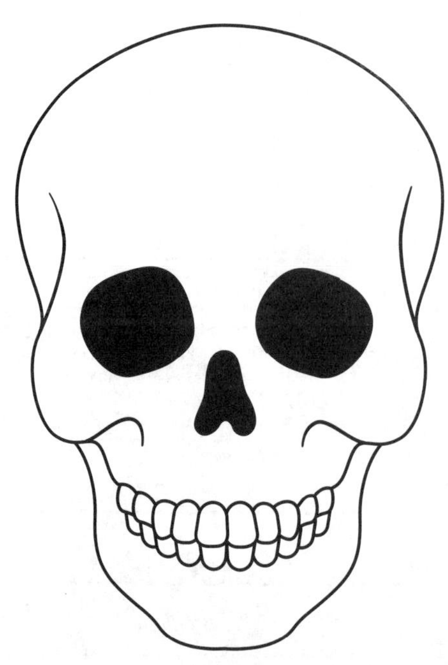

Name______________________________________

Use the passage on page 54 to complete the activity.

Read each statement. Write **F** if it is a fact or **O** if it is an opinion.

______ 1. Mallegni and his Italian team developed a computer program that helps archeologists reconstruct the faces of ancient people.

______ 2. The computer program attempts to account for cultural and historical differences in the thicknesses of muscles and skin.

______ 3. Since the computer program accounts for cultural and historical differences in the thicknesses of muscles and skin, Mallegni's team accurately rebuilds features such as lips and ears.

______ 4. Visitors to a traveling exhibit can look at Mallegni's reconstruction of the sailor's features.

______ 5. The ancient sailor was discovered near Pisa, Italy.

______ 6. The ancient sailor raised his arm to protect himself and his dog from the shifting cargo.

______ 7. The ancient sailor died clutching a dog.

______ 8. The ancient sailor's foot was tangled in rope.

______ 9. The ancient sailor looks as if he could live next door.

______ 10. The ancient sailor was about 40 when he died.

______ 11. The Egyptian soldier's skull showed a wound of the kind that might be received in a battle.

______ 12. The Egyptian soldier died of a wound received in battle.

______ 13. Mallegni believes that the ancient Roman whose face he reconstructed is the painter Giotto.

______ 14. Mallegni compared the Roman face he reconstructed to a self-portrait of the painter Giotto.

______ 15. The pattern of wear on the artist's teeth revealed that he probably often held his paintbrush between his teeth.

Name________________________________

Inference

Read the letter. Then, answer the questions on page 57.

Write Me a Letter

July 26

Dear Mrs. Boyson,

Aloha from the Big Island! This state is so beautiful! We had the chance to drive fairly close to the volcano again this week. No activity, but that's okay. The sugar cane workers of the area love the weather we've been having lately. That sure looks like hard work to me!

I've gotten to know a few more kids this past week. I'm surprised how many friends I've made in the short time I've been here since school got out in June. By the way, how are things in the North Country? Any news from the Americans to your south? And how is the exchange student my parents are hosting this summer? Her name is Rachel, right? I think it's great that someone is using my room while I'm doing the same over here. The Posts, by the way, are a great couple and their kids sure love to tell me everything about the land here. I'll bring back some good tropical specimens to share with you for school.

It's weird to think there's just a couple of years left in high school. Thanks for getting me into this program. I never thought I'd ever get to see those plants and animals you told us about in class last year. I gotta thank my parents too. I don't think it was easy for them to let their daughter out of their sight for so many weeks.

About every day we kids have a chance to kick the ol' ball around. I'm not playing fullback or goalie as much as I do for our school's team back home. Hey, did you know that these guys didn't know our city was the capital of our province? Many of them never even heard of the CN Tower or the Royal Ontario Museum. So, when they found out how much I know about this sport, they went lame. I guess they thought we only played hockey and raced dogsleds or something.

Say, before I forget, how is Ellis doing? Thanks for taking care of him while I'm gone. Dad was kinda worried about that. He said he had no clue how to care for such a critter. Now that Ellis has turned 60, his diet has changed a bit. Let me know what you think of his coloring. It seems to me his green feathers are a bit less glossy than they should be. Although I miss him and he misses me (he does call me "Lady Love," you know), I know he's in good hands. Just don't teach him too many new words. His vocabulary is already greater than that of half the sophomore class!

Write Me a Letter (continued)

I can't wait until the 12th. That's when we fly off to the Land of the Rising Sun. Wow, to think that I'll be flying clear to the other side of the world! Crazy, huh? The Posts are kinda surprised. They thought I'd be more homesick by now. And I would be, but there is so much to see here. And then, to top it all off with a flight to visit our sister city in Asia, to see Shinto shrines, Mount Fuji, another culture. I am so excited!

Tell Mom and Dad I love them. Of course, I'm writing them again tomorrow, but you know what I mean. The boys here are as shy around me as most guys are back on King Street. Kinda funny. Kids are pretty much the same wherever you go.

I'll see you next autumn. Thanks for the birthday card. Never thought you'd remember. Well, I guess I did.

With great appreciation,
Chris

Use the letter on pages 56 and 57 to answer the questions. Cite evidence from the text to support your answers.

1. Where is Chris living this summer? ____________________
2. How long has Chris been there? ____________________
3. What is the purpose of the trip? ____________________
4. Is Chris a boy or a girl? ____________________
5. What does Mrs. Boyson teach? ____________________
6. What kind of pet does Chris own? ____________________
7. Where does Chris go next? ____________________
8. Where is Chris' home? ____________________
9. What is Chris' favorite sport? ____________________
10. What activities has Chris been involved in on the trip?

____

____

____

Name________________________________

Inference

Read the passage. Then, answer the questions on page 59.

The Escape

Into the shady glen the small figure rode on a pony little larger than a dog. The pony's breath misted in the crisp air as the beast blew air out of its nostrils. The green-mantled figure patted the neck of the beast, whispering words of comfort into the animal's ear. In response, the faithful steed nickered, thumped his wide hoofs twice upon the soft bed of the forest floor, and ceased its shaking.

"We've left the raiders behind, old friend," said Ruby, as she removed her hooded mantle and tossed her head back and forth, brining peace to her own troubled mind. Ruby was not human. She was neither the elfin nor dwarf of story tales. Nay, she was a mystic, one of four daughters of Sierra, guide of all wood folk.

Suddenly shouts of rough men and screams of abused warhorses cut through the glade's peace.

"In here, ol' churl, I tell ya. The maid's gone to hidin' in this grove."

"Nah, ya lunk. She'd never wait for us here. Not after she dunked old Stephen at the marsh. Noo! She's a gone on to her crazy folk, don'tcha know."

The two grey-cloaked riders dismounted, still arguing as they examined the earth for traces of the maiden's flight.

"Who was the lout who let her escape?" asked the first.

"Tis one who no longer breathes the air so freely," returned the second grimly. "The lord beheaded the fool by scimitar even as the knave begged for mercy. Ah, there's little patience for one who lets a mystic escape, to be true!"

Five nobly dressed horsemen wove through the trees to the clearing where these two rustics still squatted. In the lead came the fierce lord, a huge form with scarlet and grey finery worn over his coat of mail.

"What say you?" he roared. "Have ye found the trail of Ruby?"

"No sire," spoke the first grey, trembling, "though I was certain the child headed into this wood. Shall I continue to search, lord?"

"Aye, indeed," replied the master calmly, controlled. "She is here, I know it too. You have a keen sense for the hunt, Miguel. Be at ready with your blade. And you too, Short Brush! Though a child, our Ruby is vicious with her weapon."

"Yes, sire," agreed Miguel and Short Brush.

The two greys beat the bushes in the search. Closer and closer they came to the child's hiding place, a small earthen scoop created when the roots of a wind-blown tree pulled free of the earth.

The evil lord and his lot remained mounted, ready to pursue should the young girl determine to take flight once more.

And so they were not prepared for the child's play.

Ruby softly, softly sang, "You wind-whipped branches shudder, shake. You oaks and cedars tremble, take these men and beasts who do us wrong. Not in these woods do they belong."

Name________________________________

The Escape (continued)

As a mighty gust of wind roared, nearby trees slapped their branches to the point of breaking, as they reached out and grasped the five mounted men. An immense gaping cavern opened in the trunk of an ancient oak and swallowed the five surprised mail-clad men whole before closing and crushing the evil ones.

Miguel and Short Brush too were lifted high into the air by a white pine and a blue spruce. Lifted high. Kept high. For awhile.

"Return from whence you came. Go to your families and tell them of the wrath of Sierra," commanded Ruby. "She would not you to her land come again!"

The pine and spruce tossed the two gray trackers over the trees of the forest and into the field beyond. A field already harvested and soggy with the rains of autumn. Miguel and Short Brush, unhurt but shaken by their **arboreal** flight, rose and fled immediately to tell their missus of the strange doings of this wood.

The child Ruby gathered the reins of her pony, climbed on to her mount, and turned her beast toward her mother's lodge, a mere three days travel.

Use the passage on pages 58 and 59 to answer the questions. Cite evidence from the text to support your answers.

1. What sort of creature is Ruby? ______________________________

2. What do you know about this creature? ______________________________

____

3. How many enemies are mentioned in this passage? ______________________________

4. How do you know of the power of Ruby? ______________________________

____

5. Infer. Why might the lord wish to recapture Ruby? ______________________________

____

6. What is the meaning of the word **arboreal**? ______________________________

7. Why might Ruby have allowed the two rustics to remain alive? ______________________________

____

8. What season of the year is it? ______________________________

Name________________________________

Inference

Read each clue. Use the names in the word bank to infer which creature is being described.

I've Got a Secret

ant	bat	blue racer	monarch butterfly	duck	frog
hummingbird	moth	opossum	pike	rabbit	spider

1. I fly in the evening to catch insects. I have large ears unlike birds. Oh, I have hair too. ____________________

2. I am a weaver. By my art I capture my food. I'll bite my victim to inject it with poison so it's paralyzed. And I'll eat my food when I'm good and ready. Or I'll let my children eat it. ____________________

3. I love to swim, but I fly very well too. My feathers keep me warm all my waddling days. ____________________

4. Most of us fly at night. We are attracted to light. We have feathery antennae and our young sit around in cocoons. ____________________

5. I have smooth, moist skin and live both on land and in water. My young have tails and must stay in water, I love insects. Humans seem to think I love lily pads. ____________________

6. My babies cling to me as I search for food. I'm hairy, but I do have a smooth, hairless tail. Some folks say I fool my enemies by faking my death. ____________________

7. I nibble greens. My wild cousins blend well with their surroundings but I'm white. I'm hairy. I walk… well, I bound really. And I live in a burrow. ____________________

8. I am a hard worker. I have six legs and two antennae. I use my mouth to carry loads, and I can carry a lot for my size. A few of my family fly but most of our large colony are wingless. ____________________

9. When I fly, my wings beat so fast that people can hardly see them. I'm larger than a bumblebee but have only two wings. I can fly backwards. ____________________

10. I flutter and fly in the sunshine. I'll land on milkweeds with all six legs and lay my eggs. ____________________

11. My sense of smell depends on my tongue. I'm scaly, not slimy! I'll swallow rodents whole and let my body digest them. I slither quickly through the grass. I shed my skin as I outgrow it. ____________________

12. It's no joke. My teeth are razor sharp, and I will attack other swimming critters. I've even chomped on birds that land on the water. I'm not fussy, just hungry! ____________________

Name________________________________

As Kaya glanced through the classified section of the newspaper last night, she came upon some rather peculiar ads. Match the ads to Kaya's comments.

In the Classifieds

_____ 1. **Chevy 1998 Cavalier**: Has all 4 tires. Runs. May need work. You haul it away yourself. $500 or best offer. Call Clutch at 555-5555.

_____ 2. **Wanted**: Tired of sitting around the house doing nothing? Well, we are looking for people who wish to earn money without leaving home. You don't even need to talk to anyone! The position calls for the stuffing of envelopes. Ask for Ito at 555-5555.

_____ 3. **Wanted**: A cool MP3 player that can play a really good cool sound. Call Kwan the Cool Man at 555-5555.

_____ 4. **Services**: I will sing for your wedding party. I know "Clementine," "I Love You Truly," "Killing Me Softly," and "Loving You." Wages negotiable. Call Kenny at 555-5555.

_____ 5. **Wanted**: Somebody to walk my dog. No references needed. Choose your days to take my mutt. Any age person may apply. See Lucky at 555-5555.

_____ 6. **Ponys' four sail**: We gots a hoarse wo had to coalts! theys reddy four a gud home. Call me att 555-5555.

_____ 7. **Lost**: My kitty. She is yellow and fluffy. And she has a collar and it has a name tag. Her name is Peaches and I want her back right now. Please find her. 555-5555

A. Oh, help! We'll take anyone!

B. Likely he's got a tin ear.

C. Here's a job for a recluse.

D. Well, maybe the telephone number is correct at least.

E. Not necessarily the most reliable way to go.

F. Okay. Keep your eyes peeled and help the little kid.

G. Can he use any other adjectivies?

Name____

Read the letter. Then, answer the questions on page 63.

A Letter Home

February 10, 1919

Dear Mother,

Well, here I am in Archangel, and the temperature is about 30 degrees below zero. Our commanding officer told us that Archangel is the largest city in the world so close to the Arctic Circle. I have no problem believing that. It seems as though we just stepped out of a time machine that has whisked us back to the Ice Age. How I miss Florida!

After I finished my basic training, I was so sure that I would be sent overseas to fight the Germans. Shows how much I know. By the time our regiment reached France, the fighting was over, and we were ordered to Russia instead.

It seems that here we've been sent into the middle of a civil war, which is still raging even though the Great War is over. I don't know how much of this you have read in the newspapers, but it's a mess. On one side are the White Russians. They are taking a heroic stand against the Bolsheviks (I hope I spelled that right). The Whites wanted to put the Tsar back on the throne. Now that the Tsar has been murdered, I'm not sure what the Whites would do if they won, but they are still fighting bravely. The Bolsheviks are called the Reds. They're the turncoats who made that deal with the Germans and backed out of the war.

What am I doing here? Our job right now is to guard a heap of supplies that were left over after the Russians withdrew from the war. It seems the brass are worried that either the Bolsheviks or the Germans will try to grab them. So here I sit, babysitting a stockpile of bullets. Sometimes I wonder if we're also here just in case our government decides we need to step in and help the White Russians. But, I'm afraid their cause is lost. From what I hear, Lenin has things pretty well under his thumb.

How is Brad? Please tell him to write. It gets lonely standing guard and staring at nothing but snow. Speaking of which, it's time for me to go on duty. I'll write again in a few days.

Love,
Drew

Name________________________________

Use the letter on page 62 to answer the questions.

1. From what point of view is this letter written?

____

2. Choose three adjectives to describe Drew. Cite evidence from the text to support your answers.

____

____

____

3. What words and phrases does Drew use to describe the White Russians that show his opinion of them?

____

____

____

4. What words and phrases does Drew use to describe the Red Russians, or Bolsheviks, that show his opinion of them?

____

____

____

5. Write a brief description of the events described in "A Letter Home." Write the description using the third person point of view.

____

____

____

____

____

Read the passage. Then, answer the questions on page 65.

Venice

Just before my family left on this trip, we bought a new television. A man from the store drove to our house in a van to deliver it. Today, in Venice, I watched a family bring home a new television set to their house. They had purchased it on the mainland. Then they hired a **wherry**—a narrow rowboat—to bring them and their new set back home. When they got to the entrance of the narrow canal where they lived, the boat docked, and the family had to carry the set down the walkway to their house.

People don't live in this city because it is modern or convenient. They live here because of its strange beauty. The network of canals and sidewalks is complicated and the water carries noises from a long distance. But around every corner is a wonderful surprise: an ancient sculpture, an old church, or a designer dress shop in which you can spend a few hours.

Cars don't exist here. There are no roads. The canals provide the venue for transportation, which is mostly by **gondolas** and **vaporettos**. The gondolas are lightweight, narrow barges that look like large canoes but serve as taxis. The **gondoliers**, professional boat operators, propel and steer these boats with single paddles. The first time I rode in a gondola, I was nervous, but only for a few minutes. Our gondolier sang and joked with us as he maneuvered our gondola through the crowded canal. I've also ridden on a **vaporetto**, a water bus. It's faster and more efficient, but it's not nearly as romantic! Vaporettos travel from station to station, just like regular city buses. When you get off the water bus, you walk...and walk, and walk! There are narrow pathways and hundreds of bridges to span the canals.

Nothing prepared me for the majesty of this city. The rows of curving buildings rise up from the canals as they have for centuries. The baroque churches tower over the smaller townhouses. Scattered boat launches and porches open right onto the water, which gives the appearance of a city filled with flooded streets. In fact, Venice was first built more than 1,000 years ago on a series of 118 islands that filled the great Lagoon of Venice. The first residents made their living by fishing in the muddy marshland. Over the centuries, from these humble beginnings grew this jewel of Italy, a city like no other on earth. I love to imagine all of the people who have traveled on these canals.

Name________________________________

Use the passage on page 64 to answer the questions.

1. In what point of view is Venice written?

   A. first person

   B. second person

   C. third person

2. If this article had been written in third person, it would most resemble

   A. a personal account of traveling in the city.

   B. a factual account of the city of Venice and its history.

   C. a review of a good hotel in Venice.

3. Who is the most likely speaker in this story?

   A. a travel agent who is recommending Venice to his customers

   B. a student traveling with her family in Italy

   C. a schoolteacher guiding a group of students in Venice

4. How do you know that the speaker appreciates Venice?

   A. The speaker talks of the city's strange beauty.

   B. The speaker talks of spending a few hours in a dress shop.

   C. The speaker talks of new television sets.

5. What is a *wherry*?

   A. a narrow rowboat

   B. a barge for carrying goods

   C. a water bus

6. What is the most unusual aspect of Venice?

   A. It has ancient churches.

   B. It has canals instead of streets.

   C. It was built more than 1,000 years ago.

7. How does the speaker first establish the difference between Venice and other cities?

   A. by describing how a family has to bring home a television

   B. by describing the gondolas and vaporettos

   C. by describing the history of Venice

8. How do you know that the speaker does not live in Venice?

   A. She says in the first sentence that she and her family are on a trip there.

   B. She is nervous the first time she gets into a gondola.

   C. A and B

Name________________________________

Vocabulary

Read the passage. Then, complete the activities on page 67.

Pop Out!

While Papa drove the blue Ford tractor **lickety-split** down the gravel road or through the field, he let Kasey, me, Tony, and Maddie ride the single-axle trailer.

We'd stand up **daredevil**, trying to keep balance while Papa drove like crazy. When somebody would fall off into the grass, the rest of us **hooted and hollered** and urged the fallen to catch up before we'd leave them behind. While he always slowed down a little, Papa had his twinkling eye and sneaky grin like maybe he'd like to have left the kid in the dust. Oh, it was fun!

We had one little trailer that was goofy. It had a built-in long toolbox that stretched out over the wagon and above the axle. The little ones loved riding in that **cubby**. Must've been dark. Dirty. Tight. Bumpier than **all get out**.

When Papa **toted** us over the farm to work, we had this game we'd play. We'd stand on the edge of the trailer. It was easy to fall off. The trailer was extra bouncy back there. And Papa seemed to hit every bump. And maybe we wanted to fall off sometimes. You know how some people try to fall?

So one day Papa got us all together to work with him. We were to haul wood to the house for the fireplace. That meant we could ride on the trailer. Kasey and I, we played daredevil standing on the back. Tony and Maddie chose to hide themselves away in that silly wooden toolbox.

The wood lot was way out across the farm. But, we had the ride of our lives. Papa drove over every bump on the way, but Kasey and me, we never fell off. Not once! The little **squeakers** howled and groaned every time Papa bounced us over a rock. Sounded like they were dying of toothaches, the way they bellowed. Papa charged over hill and dale reeling around gullies, and so on but we wouldn't fall off. Papa was impressed. There was one last steep incline and Papa **revved** up the tractor, nudging the throttle a tad. Kasey and me, balancing on the back, must have outweighed the front of the trailer because suddenly the **linchpin**, the pin holding the trailer to the tractor—well, it popped out. Then, all sorts of things happened. Papa raced along the Ford.

The trailer, when its forward force vanished, ceased its forward motion and began speeding backward in an uncontrolled manner. Kasey and I jumped off as the trailer rushed past us.

The small door to the toolbox snapped open, and a head popped out. Tony. With eyes opened wide in surprise he shot out of that box like a pea out of a shooter. Maddie followed in perfect imitation. Both fell free of the **miscreant** wagon.

We all hollered for Papa to halt. The trailer charged to the bottom of the hill and came to rest against the trunk of the apple tree. We hollered some more and Papa must've heard us. He stopped and came back to retrieve us.

We still love riding daredevil on the trailer. But I've never seen anybody pop out of a box like Tony and Maddie. Their eyes were **bugging out** like Kalamazoo.

Name________________________

Use the passage on page 66 to complete the activities.

anything you could imagine	dangerously	high-pitched little kids	quickly
metal bolt	open wide	small enclosure	sped
transport	villainous	yell loudly	

1. Use the word bank to match the words from the story to their meanings.

   a. lickety-split ________________________

   b. daredevil ________________________

   c. hoot and holler ________________________

   d. cubby ________________________

   e. all get out ________________________

   f. tote ________________________

   g. squeakers ________________________

   h. revved ________________________

   i. linchpin ________________________

   j. miscreant ________________________

   k. bugging out ________________________

2. Why does the narrator love riding in the trailer? Cite evidence from the text to support your answer.

   ____

   ____

3. What might Tony and Maddie have thought as they left the tool box?

   ____

   ____

Name________________________________

Vocabulary

Read each sentence. Find the meaning of each underlined word and place the letter of the answer in the blank.

America's Beauties

A. caves	B. mean and dangerous	C. debris
D. steep-walled	E. great and wonderful	F. hot springs of water
G. curved structures	H. beach and shore	I. low and round areas
J. waterfalls	K. type of deer	L. volcano's hole

______ 1. Sequoia National Park in California has majestic giant trees.

______ 2. Arches National Park in Utah has tall stone arches and towers.

______ 3. Big Bend National Park in Texas has high mountains and deep basins.

______ 4. Carlsbad Caverns National Park in New Mexico has millions of bats living in the caverns.

______ 5. Everglades National Park in Florida has vicious alligators.

______ 6. Yosemite National Park in California has great torrents crashing down.

______ 7. Yellowstone National Park in Wyoming has steaming geysers.

______ 8. Mesa Verde National Park in Colorado has ruins from old American Indian tribes.

______ 9. Grand Canyon National Park in Arizona has deep, sheer canyons.

______ 10. Denali National Park in Alaska has grizzly bears and caribou.

______ 11. Olympic National Park in Washington has miles of Pacific coastline.

______ 12. Lassen National Park in California has an empty crater at the top of the mountain.

Name____________________________________

Read the passage. Then, circle **true** or **false** to answer each question.

Leonardo's Way of Seeing

Leonardo da Vinci believed in **saper vedere**, or the power of observation. While his contemporaries looked for scientific truth in the writings of ancient scholars, da Vinci's theories were based on **empirical** research, that which he observed and recorded in his many notebooks.

"How does the human body work?" da Vinci asked himself. To answer this question, da Vinci learned to **dissect** cadavers—usually the bodies of dead criminals. He then made thousands of detailed sketches of their muscles, organs, and skeletons.

1. *Saper vedere* and the power of observation most likely mean the same thing.

   A. true

   B. false

2. *Empirical research* is based on observations.

   A. true

   B. false

3. When da Vinci recorded his observations, it means he made audio versions of them.

   A. true

   B. false

4. The word *cadaver* and the word criminal mean the same thing.

   A. true

   B. false

5. Leonardo da Vinci probably made sketches of the heart.

   A. true

   B. false

6. In the context of the passage, empirical means "minor."

   A. true

   B. false

7. Leonardo da Vinci conducted his research exactly like other Renaissance scientists.

   A. true

   B. false

8. To dissect something means "to cut it apart."

   A. true

   B. false

Name________________________

What words do you think of when you hear the numbered words below? Match each with its partner from the word bank. On another sheet of paper, choose five word pairs and explain what each means or represents. You may have to do a little research!

Togetherness

Clark	conquer	cheese	dance	doom
eggs	Eve	fall	foot	fro
goats	Gretel	Indian	jelly	*Odyssey*
Qs	repel	roll	subtract	saucer
shut	south	stretch	tell	there
winter				

1. open and __________
2. bend and __________
3. Hansel and __________
4. hand and __________
5. French and __________
6. song and __________
7. *Iliad* and __________
8. sheep and __________
9. bacon and __________
10. north and __________
11. Adam and __________
12. rock and __________
13. macaroni and __________
14. rise and __________
15. gloom and __________
16. summer and __________
17. Ps and __________
18. attract and __________
19. divide and __________
20. show and __________
21. Lewis and __________
22. to and __________
23. add and __________
24. peanut butter and __________
25. here and __________
26. cup and __________

Name____________________________________

Vocabulary

Look at the underlined words in the recipe. Then, circle the meaning of each word as it is used in the recipe.

Recipe for Success

Aunt Mia's Party Cake

To bake this cake, you need to acquire one fresh egg. Next, add just a dab of butter. It is absolutely critical to use exactly 237 ml of sugar. Choose a mixing gadget and mix thoroughly. Add sufficient flour; 340 ml should be enough. Gently heat 118 ml of milk to a lukewarm temperature. You can substitute water if necessary. Shake 5 ml of baking powder from its canister into the mixture. Crush 118 ml of walnuts and add. Pour the mixture into a baking pan. Sprinkle an assortment of colored candies on top. Bake at 350 degrees for one hour.

1. acquire
   - A. criticize
   - B. hand
   - C. get
   - D. match
2. dab
   - A. a lot
   - B. a little bit
   - C. a panful
   - D. a stick
3. critical
   - A. angry
   - B. necessary
   - C. unimportant
   - D. random
4. gadget
   - A. tool
   - B. type
   - C. spoon
   - D. fork
5. sufficient
   - A. a lot
   - B. a little
   - C. too much
   - D. enough
6. lukewarm
   - A. cool
   - B. tepid
   - C. hot
   - D. disinterested
7. substitute
   - A. to replace with
   - B. to continue
   - C. to return
   - D. to provide
8. canister
   - A. box
   - B. container
   - C. crate
   - D. flat
9. crush
   - A. chop finely
   - B. squeeze
   - C. crowded
   - D. slice

Name______________________________

Vocabulary

Look at the underlined words in the menu. Then, circle the meaning of each word as it is used in the menu.

Time for Lunch

• • • • • MENU • • • • •

Hamburger with a handful of potato chips	$4.00
Hamburger with scores of potato chips	$6.00
Sandwich of thinly carved turkey	$5.00
Hot dog with very hot relish	$3.50
Fresh shrimp—you discard the shells!	$7.50
An entrée of fish with mixed-greens salad	$8.00
Spaghetti cooked in a large kettle	$4.50
Salad with crunchy croutons on top	$3.50
Apple pie from a farm-fresh crop of apples	$2.50

1. handful
   A. measured by hand
   B. a small amount
   C. a large amount
   D. crushed

2. scores
   A. sheets of music
   B. a small amount
   C. a large amount
   D. ratings

3. carved
   A. cut
   B. chopped
   C. corner
   D. drawn

4. hot
   A. warm
   B. spicy
   C. burned
   D. dressed

5. discard
   A. keep
   B. merge
   C. create
   D. toss aside

6. entrée
   A. entrance
   B. main dish
   C. snack
   D. exit

7. kettle
   A. drum
   B. drawer
   C. frying pan
   D. large pot

8. croutons
   A. bread crumbs
   B. bread slices
   C. dried bread cubes
   D. toast with butter

9. crop
   A. produce supply
   B. riding equipment
   C. new plants
   D. fruit

Read. Then, circle the correct answer to complete each analogy.

Analogies

An **analogy** finds the similarities between two things that are primarily dissimilar. To do that, the analogy makes a comparison. If you were to say, "A meteor is to an astronomer as a geode is to a geologist," you would be making an analogy. You are saying that one object (the meteor) is studied by one type of scientist in a similar way that another object (the geode) is studied by a different kind of scientist. In this way, you are showing a connection between them.

1. Lava is to volcano as stalactite is to __________.

   A. moon

   B. ocean

   C. island

   D. cave

2. Moldy is to rancid as edict is to __________.

   A. eviction

   B. proclamation

   C. conviction

   D. cheese

3. Stomach is to digestion as lung is to __________.

   A. transpiration

   B. respiration

   C. dehydration

   D. circulation

4. Author is to essay as composer is to __________.

   A. orchestra

   B. fortissimo

   C. symphonic

   D. concerto

5. Milliliter is to liter as meter is to __________.

   A. kilometer

   B. centimeter

   C. millimeter

   D. decimeter

6. Quadruped is to cat as biped is to __________.

   A. human

   B. millipede

   C. dog

   D. fish

Name________________________________

Read the passage. Then, match each underlined idiom with its meaning.

Food for Thought

The waiter was taking a break outside the back door of the restaurant. He said to a brand-new employee, "You just have to be the one to break the ice with the chef. Sometimes it seems like he has a chip on his shoulder, but he's okay. But, this is a busy place. You've jumped out of the frying pan and into the fire, let me tell you. I hope you don't have any pie-in-the-sky ideas about taking things easy here. Some days, I feel like I'm going bananas. It might not be your cup of tea. I think we've got the cream of the crop here; everybody does a great job. It's hard sometimes not to fly off the handle when things are so hectic, though. In a nutshell, I think you'll do all right if you don't mind hard work."

1. ________ to break the ice
2. ________ a chip on his shoulder
3. ________ out of the frying pan and into the fire
4. ________ pie-in-the-sky
5. ________ going bananas
6. ________ your cup of tea
7. ________ the cream of the crop
8. ________ fly off the handle
9. ________ in a nutshell

A. unrealistic
B. something one enjoys
C. the best available
D. to make a start
E. to lose one's temper
F. seemingly angry or resentful
G. go crazy
H. from a bad situation to worse one
I. to sum up

Name________________________________

Vocabulary

Circle the synonym of each of the bolded words. The circled words, when put in their numbered spaces, will form sentences.

Got a Match?

1.	**wing**	arm	fly	feather	cable	(3)
2.	**oceans**	continents	lakes	vistas	seas	(6)
3.	**fowls**	pteranodons	rabbits	birds	bones	(1)
4.	**spacious**	vast	burgeon	absent	mouthful	(5)
5.	**beyond**	toward	against	across	near	(4)
6.	**noiselessly**	silently	surely	amusingly	slowly	(2)

_______ (1) _______ (2) _______ (3) _______ (4) _______ (5) _______ (6)

7.	**ascended**	mastered	shuffled	climbed	twisted	(4)
8.	**compliant**	taciturn	shy	obsolete	obedient	(2)
9.	**ancient**	hardened	transient	absolute	old	(6)
10.	**warily**	merely	cautiously	extreme	tiredly	(1)
11.	**grating**	creaky	charming	boxing	stony	(5)
12.	**benches**	stiles	spines	goals	pews	(7)
13.	**juveniles**	renegades	children	parrots	villains	(3)

_______ (1) _______ (2) _______ (3) _______ (4) _______ (5) _______ (6) _______ (7)

14.	**brawny**	dour	clean	stout	smart	(2)
15.	**determinedly**	thoughtfully	sanely	resolutely	mutely	(7)
16.	**toted**	hauled	gave	wrote	pained	(4)
17.	**cases**	shelves	levers	tops	cartons	(6)
18.	**roustabouts**	angels	chickens	grievances	laborers	(3)
19.	**a gross**	20	money	short	144	(1)
20.	**icebox**	frigid	refrigerator	cubic	storage	(5)

_______ (1) _______ (2) _______ (3) _______ (4) _______ (5) _______ (6) _______ (7)

Name________________________________

For each problem, circle the word which does not belong with the other three. Then, take the chosen letter from the circled word and place it in the blanks below to discover the mystery phrase.

London's Calling

1.	clarinet	viola	harp	piano	(1st letter)
2.	Hansel	Riding Hood	wolf	grandmother	(2nd letter)
3.	pear	plover	pickle	pumpkin	(2nd letter)
4.	trial	lawyer	align	proof	(2nd letter)
5.	bud	root	branch	bone	(2nd letter)
6.	cooperate	follow	share	harmonize	(1st letter)
7.	volleyball	football	tennis	ping-pong	(4th letter)
8.	score	gross	dozen	fifth	(5th letter)
9.	Macbeth	Lowry	Paulsen	Cleary	(5th letter)
10.	papier maché	clay	bowl	paint	(3rd letter)
11.	Libya	Lithuania	Liberia	Lisbon	(2nd letter)
12.	strait	ocean	island	bay	(3rd letter)
13.	mackerel	squid	barracuda	salmon	(5th letter)

The __ __ __ __   __ __   __ __ __   __ __ __ __

1 2 3 4   5 6   7 8 9   10 11 12 13

Challenge: Who is responsible for the mystery phrase title?

____

Name____________________________________

Context Clues

This coded letter has just been treated with onion juice by our cryptographers to enable our Washington team to read it. It contains bold printed words written with letters in disarray. Decode the letter and those words to help the government in this top-secret project. Underline information in the text that helps you to determine the mixed-up words.

Top Secret

Tara
, yours Sincerely

.week0mid by ".Inc ,Movers" from suit law a expect We .them warned I ",package the lift you when backs your **reujin** (1) ____________________ don't Please" .movers local hired We .carry to **bercumsome** (2) ____________________ too package the found We .Vegas Las to container this send and vault lined- **teeroncc** (3) ____________________ a in contaminants the seal must we decided I .ruling a make to compelled was ,leader team as ,I ,**clodaked** (4) ____________________ bitter a in team the With .discovery our about noisily **gleanwr** (5) ____________________ to began team alpha The .were they what learn to attempt an in book **feerrceen** (6) ____________________ a used We .**wlwhiirnsd** (7) ____________________ miniature like about spun creatures celled-one The !**gheenyi** (8) ____________________ proper practiced has never Edwards Fr. ,course Of .skin Edwards' Dr. invaded **atrabcei** (9) ____________________ microscopic strange ,probe our began we As .events **tracnloun** (10) ____________________ were tests our reasons obvious For .weeks recent in center control disease our to come have complaints of number **xcesvisee** (11) ____________________ An .code in you to information this pass must I ,**cruseyit** (12) ____________________ national of sake the For

:President Mrs. Dear

Name______________________________

Context Clues

Read. Then, circle the word that best completes each sentence.

Trepidation

1. Kevin slowly picked up his __________ to play the Chopin nocturne.

   toothpick   clarinet   piano

2. With fearful trepidation he lifted the mouthpiece to his __________.

   ears   chest   lips

3. Out of the bell of his reed instrument came a __________ squawk.

   horrendous   peaceful   loving

4. Mrs. Chadwick abruptly lowered her __________.

   button   shoe   baton

5. "Who so shockingly __________ in a goose from his or her barnyard? She queried.

   brought   danced   cooked

6. Feeling so __________ he could have hidden under his chair, Kevin raised his hand.

   daring   awful   sleepy

7. Forty-two pairs of eyes turned to stare at the __________-red face of this boy.

   potato   beet   celery

8. Mrs. Chadwick, noting Kevin's chagrin, calmly regained the attention of her __________.

   ears   clarinet   class

9. "Who can tell me the last time they didn't make a rude sound with a __________ instrument?" she began.

   scientific   musical   electronic

10. Mrs. Chadwick looked at every band member who __________ and nodded their heads.

    hollered   smiled   marched

Name____________________________________

Read the passage. Choose a word from the word bank to replace each underlined word.

Can It Get Any Better?

andante	carafe	gentleman	mirth	rust	adventures
demise	investigator	palpitate	turret	bellowing	detritus
jade	pretentious	bistro	flicker	mass	repel

As I sit outside a (1) small restaurant in the village of Gagne, I must share a moment of (2) laughter, recalling my recent (3) feats.

You see, I am the famous (4) researcher, Jean LeSimpe! Yes, I am the one who rediscovered the Angolan (5) woodpecker. I am the brave soul who survived the 50-foot drop from a (6) small tower outside Amsterdam. Ah, and I can see your heart is beginning to (7) throb as you recall the *Washington Post's* story of my escape from the pile of (8) loose rock fragments as a (9) large crowd of (10) superior-assuming snobs planned my (11) ruin.

Yes, as I pour myself a drink of water from this (12) glass bottle and play the (13) moderately slow movement from my beloved Verdi's *Mass*, I am indeed thankful. If not for the mysterious young (14) fellow in the (15) brown and (16) green colored topcoat who drove into the midst of that (17) screaming crowd, I would not have been able to (18) drive back their ringleaders with my trusty umbrella.

Some day I shall tell you the entire story.

1. ____________________
2. ____________________
3. ____________________
4. ____________________
5. ____________________
6. ____________________
7. ____________________
8. ____________________
9. ____________________
10. ____________________
11. ____________________
12. ____________________
13. ____________________
14. ____________________
15. ____________________
16. ____________________
17. ____________________
18. ____________________

Name________________________________

Read the passage. Then, complete the activity.

Say What?

President Kennedy once traveled to Berlin, Germany. The Berliners had suffered after World War II. President Kennedy wanted to show the bond he felt with them. He practiced saying *I am a citizen of Berlin* in German to create that bond. When the time came to speak, instead of saying *Ich bin Berliner*, as the correct translation would read, he intoned the words *Ich bin eine Berliner*. The addition of the word *eine* changed his sentence. His new sentence translated into *I am a cream-filled pastry*! Despite his political blooper, the Berliners loved him for trying.

Read the following bloopers. They are funny because the politicians used the wrong word or phrase. These wrong words are printed in bold type. Think about the context of the statement the politician was making. What word should the politician have used instead? You will find suggestions inside the parentheses that follow each sentence. Help the politician out by underlining the correct word or words. Use the dictionary if needed.

1. George W. Bush, presidential candidate, talking about people who did not take his abilities seriously enough: They **misunderestimated** me. (misunderstood, underestimated)
2. Al Gore, vice president: A zebra doesn't change its **spots**. (stripes, mind)
3. Thomas M. Menino, mayor of Boston: The (school) principals deserve the right to install **mental detectors** in their schools. (mental inspectors, metal detectors)
4. Gib Lewis, Texas House speaker: This is **unparalyzed** in the state's history: (unpasteurized, unparalleled)
5. Gib Lewis, Texas House speaker: I want to thank each and every one of you for having **extinguished** yourselves in this season. (distinguished, exterminated)
6. John King, New Hampshire Governor: I am privileged to speak at this **millstone** in the history of this college. (milestone, load)
7. George Bush, presidential candidate: I like meeting people, my fellow citizens, I like **interfacing** with them. (interfering, interacting)
8. Dan Quayle, vice president: One word sums up probably the responsibility of any vice president, and that one word is "**to be prepared**." (to be ready, preparedness)
9. Dan Quayle, vice president: It's wonderful to be here in the great **state** of Chicago. (city, country)

Name________________________________

Read. Choose a word from the word bank to complete each sentence.

Finishing Touches

grimace	polish	sparkle	comprehend	harmonize
tighten	examine	heckle	share	walk
kindle	sneeze	whimper		

1. If Sean is pitched four balls, he will ____________________.
2. Because we were so cold coming indoors on that wintry eve, Torrance brought in some wood to ____________________.
3. The silver tea set had lost its luster so Mama had me ____________________ it.
4. Because the puppy wished to go outdoors while we were all gone, she began to ____________________.
5. The four burly men with red-and-white striped shirts gathered around the piano player in order to let their voices ____________________.
6. The lab technician set the sample beneath the microscope to ____________________ the tissue sample.
7. Without the Triple Q Decoder, which he left in his glove compartment, the secret agent could not ____________________ the message.
8. As allergic as Kelsey is to cats, its no surprise that she would ____________________.
9. Feeling sorry for the child beggar, my brother cut his sandwich in half so that he might ____________________ it.
10. The wolf followed the wounded caribou for five miles in an effort to ____________________ his chosen prey.
11. The lemonade was so sour that Felicia could not help but ____________________. What a face!
12. Tisha brushes her dental work so that her teeth ____________________.
13. The juice sloshed out of the glass bottle because Shannon forgot to ____________________ its lid.

Name________________________________

Context Clues

Read the letter. Then, choose a word from the word bank to fill in each blank.

Haste Makes Waste

apparently	appreciate	civilly	complaints	contact
cosmetic	cost	entrance	finely	gouged
haste	in	inside	June	Movers
neighboring	repair	slid	slogan	Steinway

467 Poetry Lane
Cedar Rapids, IA
(1) ____________ 9

Acme Piano (2) ____________, Inc.
808 Hefty Drive
Brooklyn, NY

Dear Sirs:

I (3) ____________ your prompt attention and service as you moved our (4) ____________ piano for our family from New York City to Cedar Rapids this past April. Your (5) ____________ "No One's Faster" seems most appropriate.

However, I do have a small list of (6) ____________ to make. First, in taking our (7) ____________ tuned instrument from our apartment in upper Manhattan, your movers (8) ____________ a 6' x 12' hole in the wall rather than remove the piano through the service (9) ____________ as I had requested. Cost to me: $2,350.

Second, according to our (10) ____________ apartment dwellers and the police, the piano (11) ____________ out of your company's moving van not once but twice because your workers failed to strap it (12) ____________ place. Cost of structural (13) ____________ to piano legs: $3,200. (14) ____________ of tuning: $890. Cost to replace sounding board: $6,620. Cost of repair to piano exterior: $1,480.

Finally, in their (15) ____________ to leave our apartment, the movers (16) ____________ left an entire Acme Piano Movers uniform, socks, work shoes, and gloves (17) ____________ the piano! Cost of mental anguish: $1,200.

I hope we are able to settle this matter (18) ____________. I request that you compensate me $15,740 for damages. Should you choose to fight my claim, my lawyer will (19) ____________ you in seven days.

Sincerely,
Robert Conti

Name________________________________

Read the passage. Then, complete the activity.

Spacey Diets

Imagine that your school has the honor of ordering supplies for three astronauts' meals on an upcoming spaceflight. You're in charge of lunch on the first day.

NASA's dietician uses Venn diagrams like the one below to organize the foods needed for each meal. The dietician draws three circles, one for each astronaut. If all three astronauts wanted a lunch item, the dietician listed that item in the area where all circles overlapped. If only two astronauts wanted an item, the dietician listed that item in the area where the two astronauts' circles overlapped. If only one astronaut wanted an item, the dietician listed that item in that astronaut's circle, in an area that did not overlap with another astronaut's circle.

Complete the form by listing the number of orders of each food item needed.

_____ tropical punch
_____ lemonade
_____ orange-pineapple drink
_____ dried beef
_____ shrimp cocktail
_____ carrot sticks
_____ peach ambrosia
_____ beef steak
_____ macaroni and cheese
_____ potatoes au gratin
_____ broccoli au gratin
_____ green beans with mushrooms
_____ green beans and broccoli
_____ butter cookies
_____ chocolate pudding
_____ tapioca pudding
_____ candy-coated peanuts

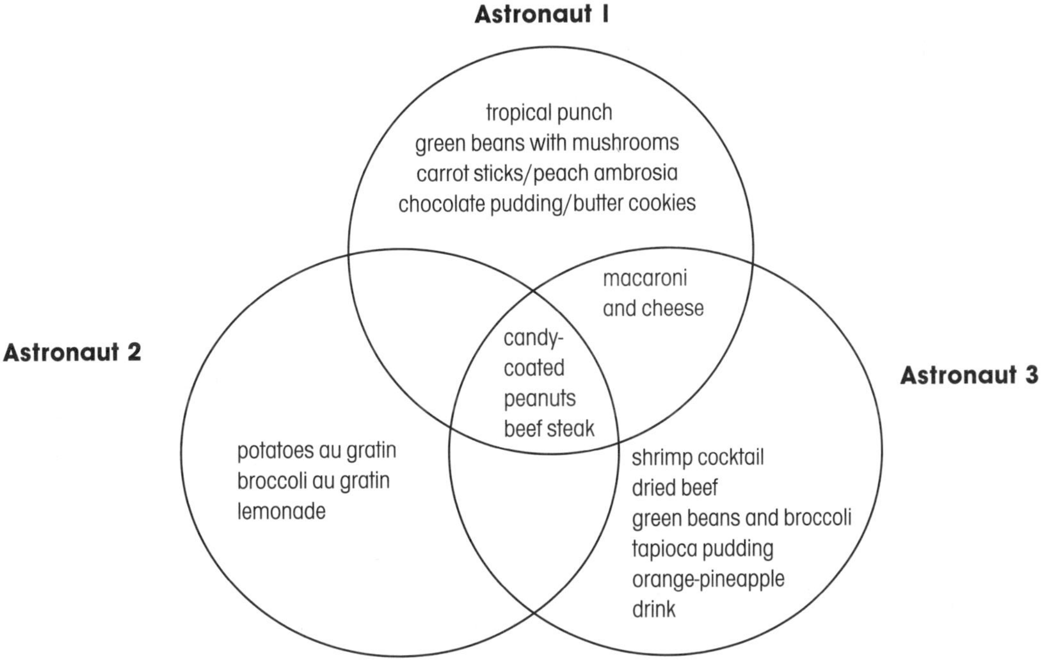

Read the tables. Then, answer the questions.

Bicycle Safety

Jenna presented a report on bicycle safety to her class. She polled her classmates about their own bicycle safety before and after her presentation. She then compiled the two frequency tables below. In her report, Jenna included safety rules and read statistics on bicycle-related injuries and deaths each year. She also pointed out that one of the most critical safety issues was wearing a helmet every time you ride a bicycle.

Safety *before* Report	**Yes**	**No**
Do you think you will always check your brakes, seat, handlebars, and tires before riding?	1	24
Do you think you will always wear a helmet?	9	16
Do you think you will always pay attention to all traffic signs?	12	13
Do you think you will regularly ride on the handlebars or with two people on a bike?	10	15
Do you think you will always walk your bike across busy intersections?	3	22
Prediction *after* Report	**Yes**	**No**
Do you think you will always check your brakes, seat, handlebars, and tires before riding?	16	9
Do you think you will always wear a helmet?	22	3
Do you think you will always pay attention to all traffic signs?	22	3
Do you think you will regularly ride on the handlebars or with two people on a bike?	2	23
Do you think you will always walk your bike across busy intersections?	22	3

1. Compare both sets of data. Write two true, specific statements comparing them. Use information from the text to support your answer.

____

____

2. Based on the data, what conclusion could Jenna make about her report?

____

3. Which details in Jenna's report may have caused the post-report results?

____

____

Name______________________________

Read the graph. Then, answer the questions.

A Far-Off Place

On the planet of Utopia, rain never falls. Hail and snow, the only two precipitation forms known there, are both common and somewhat dangerous. (This is why Utopian meteorology is a highly paid profession.) Fortunately, there are lulls in the Utopian nine-month year when citizens can enjoy the bright Rigelian sun.

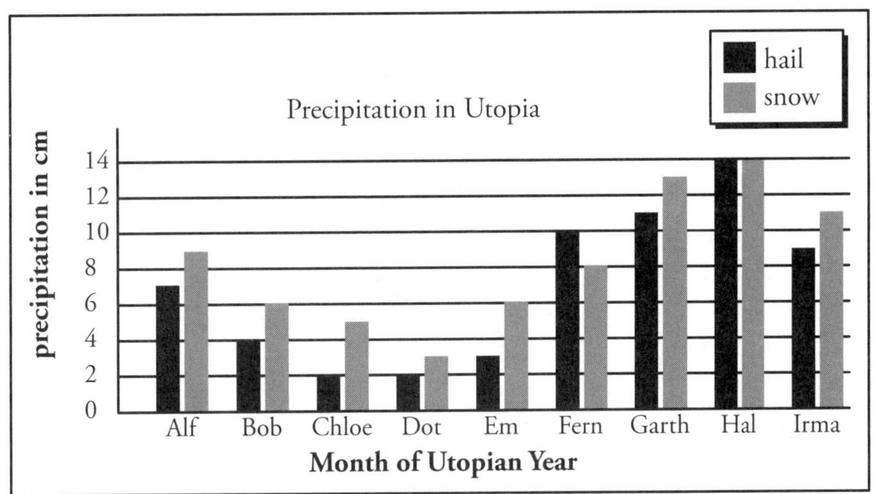

1. Which month has a total precipitation of 9 cm? ________________
2. The precipitation *always* melts within 12 hours of its accumulation. During which two months would you expect the most flooding? ________________
3. Which is normally greater, hail or snow accumulation? ________________
4. During which two months does Utopia have equal snowfall? ________________
5. If Carmon, a tourist agent, enjoys sending people on vacations when there is fewer than 10 cm of precipitation, what months would she choose? ________________
6. How much hail is expected in Fern? ________________
7. Why is the month of Fern unique? ________________
8. What is the total yearly snowfall expected on Utopia? ________________
9. What is the total yearly hail accumulation? ________________
10. Rate the months from driest to wettest. ________________

Read the article. Then, answer the questions on page 87.

Newspaper Editorial, 1890

New York City—When I returned from a tour today of the garment sweatshops on the Lower East Side, I vowed that my next editorial would be the start of a great crusade. We must do everything within our power to end this brand of oppression in America. Yes, readers, a kind of slavery still exists! It lives in the tenements of this very city, in crowded rooms and miserable hovels.

Let me take you on a tour of one of the factories I visited. Crammed into two small, dark rooms were no fewer than 20 workers hunched over ever-humming sewing machines. So intent on their work were these human automatons that they did not even notice my presence. They are paid "piece-work," which means that their only hope of staving off starvation is to complete as many sewn pieces as they can. Every finished seam adds a few more pennies to their miserable pay.

One woman paused just long enough to tell me that she never works fewer than 12 hours a day. Her workday begins at dawn and continues until 9 o'clock in the evening. Her pay? Three dollars a week, provided that she works as fast as she can the entire time.

Some of the piece-workers work in their one-room tenement apartments. There, parents and children alike crouch over a single table, sewing by hand to finish garments. Even those who fall ill in the miserable, unheated rooms must keep working or the family will go hungry.

If a sweatshop worker manages to avoid starvation, he or she may face death from disease. The poor sanitation and lack of heat and ventilation in these factories of misery offer diseases such as tuberculosis an excellent breeding ground.

How can our industry leaders justify the poor pay and working conditions of these and many other sweatshop operations? Why, I have heard them actually say that their work helps keep immigrants out of trouble and children on the straight and narrow path of virtue! Profit blinds these men to seeing justification for the horror that they themselves create.

We must rise up with one voice and say that all people, regardless of their occupation, deserve working conditions and pay that do not put their lives in danger and push their children into early graves. We must find in our hearts the ability to fight for those who are too exhausted, weak, and hungry to fight for themselves. We must do this, regardless of the fight ahead with the richest and most powerful men in this country. I challenge you, readers: speak with a factory owner that you know. Find a community leader to rally groups of people to the fight. Help the poor with your donations. If you do nothing, you will unite yourself with those who keep these miserable workers in the chains of their oppression and poverty.

Name____________________________________

Use the article on page 86 to answer the questions. Cite evidence from the text to support your answer.

1. Write a summary for this fictitious editorial. What does the writer of the editorial view as the central conflict that he is trying to confront?

2. What argument does the author make about sweatshops? What evidence is used to support this argument?

3. What challenge does the writer make at the end of the editorial to his readers?

4. What potential conflict could occur if the readers of the editorial take up the writer's challenge?

5. How does the author distinguish his/her point of view from the point of view of the factory owners?

6. Imagine this editorial was read by the factory owners and community leaders. How do you think they would respond?

Read the passage. Then, answer the questions on page 89.

Lincoln's Dream

About ten days ago, I retired very late. I had been up waiting for important dispatches from the front. I could not have been long in bed when I fell into a slumber, for I was weary. I soon began to dream. There seemed to be a death-like stillness about me. Then I heard subdued sobs, as if a number of people were weeping. I thought I left my bed and wandered downstairs. There the silence was broken by the same pitiful sobbing, but the mourners were invisible. I went from room to room; no living person was in sight, but the same mournful sounds of distress met me as I passed along. I saw light in all the rooms; every object was familiar to me; but where were all the people who were grieving as if their hearts would break? I was puzzled and alarmed. What could be the meaning of all this? Determined to find the cause of a state of things so mysterious and so shocking, I kept on until I arrived at the East Room, which I entered. There I met with a sickening surprise. Before me was a catafalque, on which rested a corpse wrapped in funeral vestments. Around it were stationed soldiers who were acting as guards; and there was a throng of people, gazing mournfully upon the corpse, whose face was covered, others weeping pitifully. "Who is dead in the White House?" I demanded of one of the soldiers.

"The President," was his answer, "he was killed by an assassin." Then came a loud burst of grief from the crowd, which woke me from my dream. I slept no more that night; and although it was only a dream, I have been strangely annoyed by it ever since.

—Account of a dream of Abraham Lincoln's. It was written down by Ward Hill Lamon, who heard President Lincoln give this account to a group of friends a few days before he went to Ford's Theater to see *Our American Cousin*.

Name________________________________

Use the passage on page 88 to answer the questions.

1. Foreshadowing is an indication of something that is going to happen. What event does Lincoln's dream foreshadow?

   A. the death of John F. Kennedy

   B. Lincoln's own assassination

   C. the death of Lincoln's son

   D. the death of Lincoln's wife

2. How long before his assassination did Lincoln have this dream?

   A. about ten days before

   B. about three days before

   C. about two weeks before

   D. about one month before

3. Which elements of this dream indicate foreshadowing?

   A. Lincoln had been waiting for reports from the front.

   B. Lincoln sees a corpse which soldiers tell him is the body of the president.

   C. All of the rooms are lighted and familiar-looking.

   D. Lincoln sees the spirit of his dead son in the East Room.

4. Dreams are one type of foreshadowing. Which of these would be another type of foreshadowing?

   A. someone feeling a sudden chill right before hearing bad news

   B. a dog barking without any reason

   C. a mother warning a child to dress warmly for school

   D. All of the above

5. *Lincoln's Dream* is from a historical account. Which of these is a foreshadowing event in fiction?

   A. Hansel and Gretel arrive at the witch's house.

   B. The ghost of Hamlet's father warns Hamlet about his uncle.

   C. Laura Ingalls Wilder moves to Dakota Territory with her family.

   D. Oliver Twist learns from Fagin how to pick pockets.

Read the passage. Then, complete the activities on page 91.

Contemplating Color

It's 101 degrees outside and your house doesn't have air conditioning. Do you dive into a pool? Do you drink glass after glass of ice water? You might want to sit very quietly in a room that is painted blue. Scientific studies have shown that people feel cooler in blue rooms than in rooms that are painted red or pink. This fact could explain why, over centuries, different colors have been used to symbolize human emotions or characteristics. Perhaps our physical reaction to color has helped explain how these symbols came to be. The color blue causes people to relax and their heart rates to slow down. Blue has often been used to symbolize tranquility and calm. But, it also is linked with depression, or "the blues." That's because that blue room might be a peaceful haven for a time, but if you spend too much time there, you can start feeling depressed or sad.

Let's look at red. All you have to do is think of Valentine's Day to know that red symbolizes love and passion in Western culture. But, did you know that the color red actually speeds up a person's breathing and increases the heart rate? That reaction could be the very thing that linked the color and the emotion of falling in love in the first place.

When you think of purple, do you think of royalty? For centuries, purple was the color of kings and queens. There was a practical reason for this originally: purple was the most costly of all dyes, and only those with tremendous wealth could afford purple cloth. In color studies, purple has been found to be the favorite color of people who are creative and intuitive—qualities that the best of rulers have had in both history and legend. So again, there may be a physical, scientific link to the ongoing symbol.

Black is another color with strong symbolism. In Western culture, we associate it with death, mystery, and evil. Black is the color that Europeans have used for mourning. In the nineteenth century, people whose spouse or child died were expected to wear black clothing for a set period of time to symbolize their loss. Farther back in time, we find black associated with evil, perhaps because it is also the color that represents night, a time when people were frightened of attacks, robberies, or even a visit from a ghost or witch.

Green is a color we associate with nature, springtime, and fertility. In medieval Europe, brides used to wear green dresses to show their hope that they would have many children. It's not surprising that we link green with nature; when you look outside, green is one of the most prominent colors in most natural settings. And the healing properties of nature convey themselves through the color green—it has a healing and soothing effect on people who are ill, which is why many hospitals choose the color for patients' rooms.

Symbols concerning color have ancient roots. When we look at the scientific and cultural links to various colors, suddenly the symbolism itself makes more sense.

Name________________________________

Use the passage on page 90 to complete the activities. Fill in the chart. For number 6, choose another color and decide on its symbolism and where it could be used.

Color	Symbol	Use
1. blue		
2. red	love and passion	
3. green		hospital rooms
4. black		
5. purple		
6.		

7. What contrasting feelings are related to the color blue?

____

____

8. If you were making a banner to symbolize a new beginning, what color would you make it? Why?

____

____

9. Why does the passage say red could be linked to falling in love?

____

____

10. How does the author organize the text?

____

____

____

Read each sentence. Match each situation with the mood it suggests.

In the Mood

A. domineering B. interested C. timorous D. weary

_____ 1. Sixteen hours of babysitting with no sleep! And that baby… was she awake again? Ohhh!

_____ 2. Man, was he ever going to get this team in shape! Ryan, captain of the team, knew he had great ideas!

_____ 3. Tara eavesdropped as her parents discussed what she hoped would be the best vacation of the century.

_____ 4. Required to speak in front of a huge audience, Brandon's knees knocked, his face reddened, and his voice croaked.

A. electrified B. lackadaisical C. skeptical D. somber

_____ 5. Well, thought John, I suppose I could help Mom with the garbage. But not now. Maybe in a couple of days.

_____ 6. Now! Is my teacher really Mr. Roger's nephew? Naw!

_____ 7. The gang was silent. They had just heard that Danielle's sister had been in a horrid accident.

_____ 8. Another point is scored! The crowd is going wild!

A. chagrined B. sluggish C. upbeat D. whimsical

_____ 9. The ninth-grade boys put on flowery hats and sat down at small tables for their dubious tea party.

_____ 10. Penny had been down with the flu for three days. She felt as though she couldn't move!

_____ 11. "Hey, what a great day!" shouted Uma. "The sky is clear and I feel wonderful!"

_____ 12. Gavin looked into the mirror, only to discover that he still had toothpaste on his nose from that morning.

Name________________________________

Critical Thinking

Read each description. Then, complete the activity.

Brothers and Sisters

Six children named Aaron, Becca, Carla, Greg, Harry, and Irene are playing in the Wagner's yard. Name the three Wagner children and list their ages.

1. If Irene isn't a Wagner, Becca is.
2. A Wagner girl is older than her brother by two years.
3. The girl, Carla, is 11.
4. If Aaron is a Wagner, Harry is.
5. If Carla isn't a Wagner, Greg isn't a Wagner.
6. A Wagner boy is older than his sister by one year.
7. Irene is Greg's sister.
8. Carla is the oldest child in her family.
9. Harry is 10.
10. The youngest of the six children is 9.

Child's Name	Age
______________________________	_____
______________________________	_____
______________________________	_____

Read each case. Then, complete the activity.

Three Cases

1. Darrell Dolby, a doting father, had three penniless children. He pulled out 60 dollars and divided it among them. The first received half the money, the second got three-tenths of the money, and the third acquired one-fifth. A swindling uncle contrived to obtain four dollars from each child, claiming that he required wart surgery. Luckily, soon after this rip-off each child found a sum of money, one in the parking lot, one in a school locker, and the third in a bag of potato chips. The amount each found was equivalent to one-half the money, which he or she still held. How much does each child have now?

	Fraction	**$**	**-$4**	**+1/2$**	**New total**
first					
second					
third					

2. Lynn Locklear, an ecology-minded landowner planted five trees: a larch, a white pine, a cedar, a hemlock, and a spruce. She noted that the trees were of five different heights. The spruce was taller than the pine but shorter than the cedar. The larch and the hemlock were neither the two tallest trees nor the shortest. The only conifer to shed its leaves (needles) yearly was of median height. Place the trees in order from tallest to shortest.

____

____

____

____

____

3. Bob, Rob, and Robert are of three generations of the Robinson family. In some order, they are grandparent, parent, and child. Bob is the parent of at least one of the others. Robert has neither father nor son. Rob has a mother. How are the three related? Hint: One of the three is a woman.

Name	Relation
____________________	____________________
____________________	____________________
____________________	____________________

Name________________________________

Read each clue. Then, complete the activity.

Oops! Sorry!

Greg has planned a Friday night party for boys and girls. Each boy was to bring a snack. As Greg knew, each boy had a crush on one of the girls invited and so brought a snack she would like. The girls reciprocated the affection. Unfortunately, the five invited boys accidentally spilled their snacks on their sweethearts. Can you match the boys, girls, and spilled snacks? Use the grid below to help you reach your decision.

	Felicia	Ginny	Holly	Ivy	Jan	chips	soda	cookies	carrots/ celery	pretzels
Andrew										
Bill										
Chase										
Dion										
Edgar										
chips										
soda										
cookies										
carrots/ celery										
pretzels										

	Boy	Girl	Snack
1.	________	________	________
2.	________	________	________
3.	________	________	________
4.	________	________	________
5.	________	________	________

1. Either Ivy or Ginny had cookie crumbs plastered on her clothes.
2. Edgar, who does not adore Felicia, did not bring cookies.
3. Pretzels or chips are the desire of Bill's heartthrob.
4. Either Felicia likes Dion or Dion's match likes soda, but not both.
5. Andrew and Chase like Ginny and Holly but not necessarily in that order. Andrew's crush loves soda.
6. Jan adores celery and carrots.
7. Ivy, who won't touch chips or cookies, is not dreaming of Edgar.

Name________________________________

Read the passage. Then, answer the questions.

Dogs Don't Go to Yellowstone

Your family plans a trip to Yellowstone National Park. You want to take your dog. He is a big, athletic dog and he will love the outdoors. You are surprised when a friend tells you about Yellowstone's rules. Review the rules your friend tells you:

> Rangers will not allow pets anywhere in the backcountry or on trails and boardwalks.
>
> Owners cannot leave pets unattended or leashed to any object. Owners have to clean up after their dogs.

Before your friend dashes off to his soccer game, he tells you that the rules are meant to protect the park, visitors to the park, wildlife, and your pet. He does not have time to tell you more.

1. List two ways pets might disturb the natural area or the wildlife at Yellowstone.

   ____

   ____

2. List one way pets might disturb other park visitiors.

   ____

3. List two ways pets might become endangered in a natural park.

   ____

   ____

Read each sentence. Write **possible** or **not possible**.

4. Since all mammals can contract rabies, visiting pets might spread rabies or other illnessess to park wildlife or pick up illnesses from them. ____________________

5. An escaped pet might have difficulty surviving in the wild. ____________________

Name________________________________

Read the article. Then, answer the questions.

Farmer Questions Chicken IQ

The Disassociated Press

HENGAARD, North Dakota – A poultry farmer in this remote community 50 miles west of Bismarck made a startling discovery last Thursday as he inspected one of his hen coops. His chickens were raising their own livestock.

"In one corner of the coop, the biddies had set up a box of beetles," said Ben Daniels. "I guess they've fed them (beetles) grain from their own mix. Can't say I ever saw anything like it before. No, this is a real corker."

According to Shannon Shaw, inspector for the state agriculture administration, the chickens had also developed a cockroach ranch, an ant colony, and a mealworm pit. When asked how long the hens had farmed these smaller creatures, Ms. Shaw offered no comment. Neither would she comment when asked about the intelligence of the chickens.

Mr. Daniels believes that the chickens are able to build the insect pens with their beaks, coordinate community goals, and plan insect harvests. He says, "The chickens are raising the bugs for food. No doubt about it. I've seen them herd them, separate the fattened critters, and gobble them down like they were having a feast." Records show that egg production in this coop has improved by 23 percent in the past 18 months, far above the production of the other coops.

When asked how smart his flock was, Daniels smiled and shrugged his shoulders. "Don't know for sure, but can't be as smart as some folks around here. You know there's been talk of an alien landing around these parts..."

1. Two people are interviewed in this article. Who are they?

   ____

2. What is the main idea of this article?

   ____

3. What is the setting of this article?

   ____

4. What three claims did the farmer make about the chickens?

   ____

5. To what does the farmer compare the chicken's intelligence?

   ____

Read the passage. Then, answer the questions on page 99.

A Visit to Green Island

The house was just before us now, on a green level that looked as if a huge hand had scooped it out of the long green field we had been ascending. A little way above, the dark, spruce woods began to climb the top of the hill and cover the seaward slopes of the island. There was just room for the small farm and the forest; we looked down at the fish-house and its rough sheds, and the weirs stretching far out into the water. As we looked upward, the tops of the first came sharp against the blue sky. There was a great stretch of rough pasture-land round the shoulder of the island to the eastward, and here were all the thick-scattered gray rocks that kept their places, and the gray backs of many sheep that forever wandered and fed on the thin sweet pasturage that fringed the ledges and made soft hollows and strips of green turf like growing velvet. The air was very sweet; one could not help wishing to be a citizen of such a complete and tiny continent and home of fisherfolk.

The house was broad and clean, with a roof that looked heavy on its low walls. It was one of the houses that seemed firm-rooted in the ground, as if they were two-thirds below the surface, like icebergs. The front door stood hospitably open in expectation of company, and an orderly vine grew at each side; but our path led to the kitchen door at the house-end, and there grew a mass of flowers and greenery, as if they had been swept together by some diligent garden broom into a tangled heap: there were portulacas all along the lower step and straggling off into the grass, and clustering mallows that crept as near as they dared, like poor relations. I saw the bright eyes and brainless little heads of two half-grown chickens who were snuggled down among the mallows as if they had been chased away from the door more than once, and expected to be again.

Excerpted from *The Country of the Pointed Firs* by Sarah Orne Jewett

Name________________________________

Use the passage on page 98 to answer the questions.

1. Which of these is an example of a simile?

   A. the gray backs of many sheep

   B. clustering mallows that crept as near as they dared, like poor relations

   C. the bright eyes and brainless little heads of two half-grown chickens

   D. the tops of the first came sharp against the blue sky

2. Which of these is an example of personification?

   A. strips of green turf like growing velvet

   B. a roof that looked heavy on its low walls

   C. we looked down at the fish-house and its rough sheds

   D. the dark, spruce woods began to climb the top of the hill

3. Which two color words are used more than once in this setting description?

   A. green and blue

   B. blue and gray

   C. green and gray

   D. blue and black

4. If you were not told that this setting was a farm, what clue would indicate that it was?

   A. the vines growing on either side of the door

   B. the fish-house and sheds

   C. the low, clean-looking house

   D. the chickens near the kitchen door

5. What is the author's purpose in the use of the similes, personification, and descriptive adjectives?

   ____

Name________________________________

Read the passage. Then, answer the questions on page 101.

One Small Light

"Chang! Chang, where are you?" called Lee. Only the October wind called back, its mournful sobbing echoing in Lee's ears. She stood on a slippery rock that jutted up from the black sea. She could not see her brother's fishing boat, and the storm had been raging for nearly an hour. Lee was afraid.

She knew that if Chang could see a light, however small, it would help him guide the boat back toward shore. The young girl had a small oil lamp and two matches she had taken from the boat. She blocked the wind with her body and tried to light the lamp. The first match sparked but then went dark in a gust of wind. Lee took the second match in her shaking fingers. A small flame bloomed. Lee leaned toward the lamp, but a blast of wind stole the tiny flame from her.

Filled with despair, the girl fought back tears. Then she remembered the whistle her father had given her long ago, before he had died. She pulled it from her pocket and put it to her lips. Lee blew with all her might. The shriek of the whistle pushed against the wind. She blew again, and the whistle sounded even louder. But, a large wave crashed against the rocks and knocked Lee into the water. She fought her way back to the rock but when she climbed to safety, she found that the whistle was gone.

Lee scanned the horizon desperately. She saw nothing but the storm-tossed waves. As a last resort, she tried calling her brother's name. "Chang!" She waited and strained to hear something, anything, over the wind. "Chang!" Suddenly, Lee felt small and helpless. She sat down on the rock and hid her face in her arms. Her body shook as she cried.

She lifted her head to wipe away her tears, and a small light blinked at her. She stood up and stared, but saw nothing. Then, a light out on the sea blinked. The waves rose and fell, and she saw the light again and again. Her heart began to pound with joy. The light was her brother's mast light. His boat had made it through the storm. Lee began to shout again. After a moment, she heard Chang's voice over the noise of the storm. All was well. Chang was headed toward shore.

Name________________________________

Use the passage on page 100 to answer the questions.

1. What is the setting of the story? How does the setting affect the story?

____

____

2. Who are the characters?

____

____

3. What is the main character's problem?

____

4. What events happen to keep the main character from getting what she wants?

   First: ____

   Second: ____

   Third: ____

5. How is the main character's problem solved?

____

6. What is the final scene of the passage?

____

7. In the first paragraph, the author says, "Only the October wind called back, it's mournful sobbing echoing in Lee's ears." What kind of figurative language is this? What does it mean?

____

____

8. Why do you think that Lee is so worried about Chang? Who will take care of Lee if Chang is lost at sea?

____

____

Read the passage. Then, complete the activities on page 103.

Vacation

We were in school, but not in school. That is to say, our bodies were at our desks but our minds had traveled ahead to Friday. Friday was the last day of school before vacation. We stared out the window at the gray sky, sending all of our energy to the clouds. "Snow!" we commanded them. "Snow, please snow!"

At home, there were lots of secret conversations. Mom whispered to our big sister. Dad whispered on the phone to Grandma. We could also hear the rustling of wrapping paper coming from the home office. We knew there were packages somewhere in the house, gifts with our names on them, but my brother and I could not find them. So we sat in the living room, watching one silly holiday special after another. Out in the kitchen, pies were baking. Cookies were baking. The scents of vanilla and almonds tormented us. But, everything was for Saturday when the grandparents, aunts, uncles, and cousins would start arriving. I munched gloomily on some salty pretzels instead.

Under my bed, I had hidden my own gifts for everyone. I had saved money for weeks to buy my mother a soft, silky scarf. My brother was getting a computer game. I had made presents for some of my cousins and my grandmother. Late at night, I would gaze up at the clear, starry sky, waiting for the first snowflakes. It had not snowed yet that year.

Thursday was the longest day of my life. Every time I looked at the black-and-white clock, only a minute or two had passed since my last look. I fidgeted through English, yawned through math, tapped my fingers through science, and gnawed my pencil during a history test. Still no school bell. Still no snow.

On Friday, we had a holiday party in class. It was a relief to get up and move around. The classroom was decorated with giant snowflakes and white crêpe paper. This was ironic, because there was still no snow. I hovered near the windows, sipping my tart red punch and glancing outside. I pressed my hand against the windowpane. It felt cold enough to snow. Why wasn't it snowing?

The last bell sounded both shrill and sweet. We bolted into the hallways. My brother and I met up at the stairs. We charged down the green stairwell, down the brown-tiled lobby, and onto the front steps of the school. We stood there for a moment. Lazy, white flakes were drifting down from the sky. The grass was already wearing a white disguise.

I imagined our home, covered in snow, the windows glowing with yellow light. On Saturday, we would build snow forts and have a massive snowball battle, with all the cousins and several of the uncles. The house would glint in the sun, wearing its heavy cap of snow.

Name________________________________

Use the passage on page 102 to complete the activities.

1. What are the two settings for this text? How do these settings impact the passage?

____

____

____

2. Write a one-sentence description of each setting, based on details from the text.

____

____

____

3. In what month is this story probably set? How do you know?

____

4. Write a two- to three-sentence description about the party that will occur on Saturday.

____

____

____

5. The author uses many words to create imagery that appeals to the five senses. Fill in the chart with two examples of each. The first one has been done for you.

	Detail 1	**Detail 2**
Sight	gray clouds	
Sound		
Taste		
Smell		
Touch		

Read the passage. Then, complete the story map on page 105.

Camping Cousins

Alfonso was the most amazing person in all of Minneapolis, and he was my cousin. By the age of 19, Alfonso was a star hockey player at the University of Minnesota. He had just earned the rank of Eagle Scout. I wanted to be exactly like him. So when Alfonso asked me to go with him on a spring fishing trip in northern Minnesota, I was elated!

After planning the trip, we gathered gear and supplies and embarked on our great adventure. We reached the Superior National Forest in northern Minnesota by early evening. We slipped our loaded canoe into the sparkling water and paddled straight to our campsite. We set up camp as the sun was setting and talked about our plans for fishing the next day.

Alfonso, the former Boy Scout, knew all the tricks of an experienced wilderness camper. After we gathered enough wood from the forest floor, he started the campfire using only flint and steel—no matches. For supper, we feasted on freeze-dried buffalo, wild rice, beef jerky, and pea soup. I ate greedily after all that work.

Exhausted, we crawled into our sleeping bags early. Alfonso entertained me with tales of past camping adventures. We were still talking quietly when a sudden north wind picked up, the temperature dropped, and it began to snow. Always alert and innovative, Alfonso found a way to increase the temperature inside the tent. He dragged a log from the woods to the opposite side of the campfire, and laid it across some rocks so it would be off the ground. Then he wrapped aluminum foil around the log. The heat from the fire reflected off the foil and into the tent. Soon images of lake trout were filling my dreams.

The snow had stopped, but sometime later a powerful wind must have kicked up the flames of our dying fire. I was still engrossed in dreams of a 20-pound fish when I was abruptly awakened by Alfonso. A spark had ignited our tent, and flames were engulfing it. Frightened, I bolted out the tent opening. The tent collapsed with Alfonso inside. Without any thought of endangering myself, I reached into the burning tent, grabbed him, and dragged him to the icy lake. We were relieved to find that we were not seriously hurt.

Later, as we stood by the blazing tent to keep warm, we considered our predicament. We were in the middle of nowhere, wearing only underwear, with our supplies grilled into ashes. Even Alfonso was unsure what to do next.

Suddenly, we heard a noise in the forest. Anxiously we listened and stared into the darkness. An all-terrain vehicle appeared on the forest trail. A ranger had spotted the light from the fire and had come to investigate. We jumped into the warm vehicle and the forester drove us to the ranger station, where we were given clothes and were able to call our parents.

Alfonso and I had many more camping adventures, but it was on this trip that Alfonso began to treat me more like a friend and equal, rather than a younger cousin. Our friendship continues to this day.

Name________________________________

Use the passage on page 104 to complete the story map and answer the question. Cite evidence from the text to support your answer.

Characters: ______________ **Setting:** Time ______________

______________ Place ______________

Events:

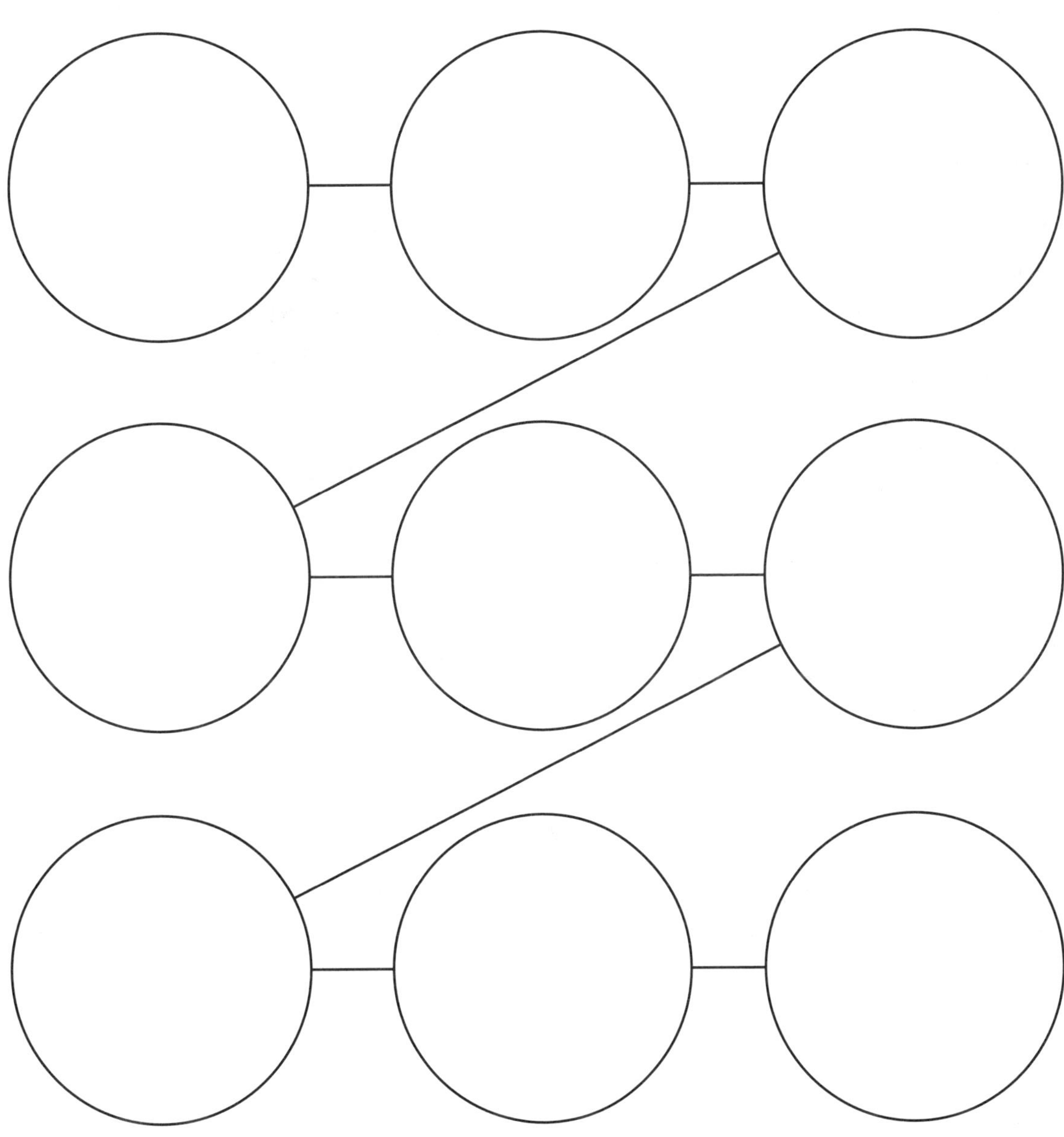

How does the relationship between the narrator and his cousin change after this camping trip?

____

____

Name________________________________

Read the passage. Then, answer the questions on page 107.

Visiting Aunt Reba

The landscape changed dramatically as we drove south. The high desert spread out before us as we made our way to Aunt Reba's house. Once or twice a year, our family drives out to Aunt Reba's century-old adobe house in a small New Mexico town. We love to visit her and help her with the ongoing restoration of the historic home she bought five years ago. Even though I sometimes dislike doing chores at home, everything seems different at Aunt Reba's house. With her good humor and laughing face, she has a way of making chores seem like a game.

As we drove up to the house, Aunt Reba came out to greet us, a big smile on her face. The reddish brown house is two stories tall. It has five rooms, including a huge central dining room. We all trooped into that room and sat around the old, planked table while Aunt Reba gave us lunch: a spicy salad topped with cheese and olives.

After lunch, we talked about the chores that needed doing during the week. "Luis will be babysitting the vegetables," Aunt Reba joked. Every time we visit, I am put in charge of the garden. I love working with the growing plants. Depending on the season, I either plant seeds, weed, or harvest vegetables. There isn't much weeding to do, since few weeds survive at this high elevation. Watering, however, is a big job. The water must be hauled from the well, and the plants have to be watered every day. Because I do this work on our visits, Aunt Reba is freed up to work with my parents on bigger repair jobs.

Maggie usually helps to chop and haul firewood. She piles the firewood neatly by the back door and then brings some into the dining room. Aunt Reba uses this wood to keep a fire going in the kiva, a special, rounded fireplace in the corner. On this trip, though, she painted a room downstairs that Aunt Reba uses as an office.

That night, after an afternoon of work, we made our evening meal. Our favorite dinner is Aunt Reba's homemade vegetable soup, served with tortillas. We sat on the bancos, or built-in benches, long after we finished eating. We laughed and joked and made plans to visit our friends in town during the week. Aunt Reba told us the Garcias were planning a cookout to celebrate our visit. Time goes quickly at Aunt Reba's house because we work hard and have such a good time in each other's company.

Name________________________________

Use the passage on page 106 to answer the questions. Cite evidence from the text to support your answers.

1. What happens first in the story?

   A. Luis's family eats lunch with Aunt Reba.

   B. Luis's family drives across the high desert.

   C. Luis's family arrives at Aunt Reba's house.

   D. Luis goes to work in the garden.

2. What happens in the middle of this story?

   A. The family eats lunch with Aunt Reba.

   B. The family spends the afternoon working.

   C. The family eats dinner.

   D. The family visits friends.

3. What makes this trip to Aunt Reba's the same as always?

   A. The family will be celebrating a holiday together.

   B. The family will take Aunt Reba visiting.

   C. The family will be helping to repair Aunt Reba's house.

   D. Luis will be chopping and stacking firewood.

4. What makes this trip to Aunt Reba's different than usual?

   A. Luis will be working in the garden.

   B. Maggie will be chopping firewood.

   C. Luis's parents will be helping Aunt Reba with a project.

   D. Maggie will be painting a room.

5. Why does this story seem like part of a larger story?

   A. because we only read about the first day of the visit

   B. because the family arrives to help Aunt Reba with chores

   C. because Luis is unhappy about the visit

   D. because we don't know what Aunt Reba was doing before the family arrived

6. What clues in the story indicate that Aunt Reba's house does not have heat and plumbing?

   ____

   ____

   ____

7. Think of the last time you visited a friend or relative, even for a few hours. On a separate sheet of paper, write the beginning, middle, and ending of your visit.

Read the journal entries. Then, answer the questions on page 109.

Gerardo's Journal

Our voyage has begun. I wish now that I had not signed on to this ship for this dreadful journey. All seemed well when we were loading our supplies and making the usual preparations. But now, a month later, I fear a curse has fallen over this ship. Only three days after we left, our mast was damaged. The *Santa María* and the *Niña* helped us get to port for repairs. The *Pinta* was seaworthy again after a few weeks. Now, we sail into the west day after day. The men whisper among themselves. They tell tales of terrible monsters who are waiting to devour our ship when we arrive at the edge of the ocean. I am fearful of these savage sea creatures, and just as fearful of the never-ending sea and the man who seems to believe we can find land where no land exists.

Our situation worsens, but there may be a small hope of saving ourselves. For days now, the crew has grown more and more vocal about how long we have sailed without seeing anything but water, stretching in all directions. Finally, some of the older sailors went to Captain Perez with their fears. He spoke directly to the Lord Admiral himself. Afterward, our three ships changed direction to the southwest. I pray that this shift in direction will keep us from sailing off the edge of the world. A rumor has it that we will try this heading for a few days only, and then turn back. I may never go to sea again, should I be fortunate enough to find my way safely home.

A miracle has occurred. Señor Garcia saw a large piece of driftwood yesterday afternoon. Amid great excitement, Captain Perez examined it. He said that since the wood was not smooth, it could not have been in the water for long. Then, early this morning, the lookout on the *Santa María* spotted some birds. The crew did their work feverishly, scanning the horizon at every other moment. Finally, we heard our own lookout's cry, the one we had waited for every day. "Land! Land!" There it was, green and hazy on the horizon under a bank of low clouds. Not monsters, but land!

Name________________________________

Use the journal entries on page 108 to answer the questions.

1. This is a fictitious journal, but it describes a historic voyage. Choose three words or phrases to describe Gerardo, the fictitious seaman who is the "author" of the journal.

___

___

___

2. What are two of Gerardo's concerns on his sea voyage?

___

___

3. There are no dates on these journal entries. When were they written? How do you know?

___

___

___

4. Why were the birds and the driftwood so heartening to the crew?

___

___

5. How do the men interact on the ship during the voyage?

___

___

6. Imagine that Gerardo goes back home after the adventure that is ahead of him. Do you think he will go back to sea again, as he wrote, or not? Give reasons for your answer.

___

___

___

Name______________________________

Sequencing

Read the two scenes. Unfortunately, the events for each scene are out of order. Number the events **1 - 7** in correct chronological order.

Time is on Your Side

Scene 1: Sandra, the social butterfly, wants to throw a party. This is what should happen these last two days:

________ write down the names of kids to invite to the party

________ take out a pen and paper

________ remind guests what time to come

________ mom said it was time to plan a guest list

________ show list to and get okay from Dad

________ number this paper from one to ten

________ call guests to invite them to the party

Scene 2: Brad, the boisterous basketball bad-boy, was warned by the coach to be ready for practice today. Strangely enough, Brad is. He did the following:

________ retrieved clothes from locker

________ remembered (for once) to take gym bag to school

________ stashed bag in locker

________ emptied the clothes drier of sports clothes in evening

________ changed into gym clothes

________ stayed awake for all classes to avoid detentions

________ packed gym bag to take tomorrow

Name________________________________

Read the poem. Then, answer the questions.

Ballad of a Cherry Pie

We met by yonder cherry tree.
I glanced at her, she winked at me.
I offered her a slice of pie.
How could I know our love would die?

After a bite, her watery eyes
Gazed at me; she gave a cry
And gagged; she turned and ran away.
I have not seen her since that day.

You see, I like my pie with spice.
Chili powder tastes so nice!
But my love I lost, so now I cry…
Say, would you like a piece of pie?

by Norm Sneller

1. What makes this poem a ballad?

   A. the rhyme scheme

   B. the fact that it tells a story

   C. the rhythm of the poem

   D. the imagery

2. What is the poet's intent in this ballad?

   A. to tell a tragic tale

   B. to question the nature of love

   C. to present the story of a historical event

   D. to create a humorous version of the ballad form

3. Why did the speaker lose his love?

   A. because the woman ran away

   B. because he gave her pie with chili powder in it

   C. because he gave up love for baking

   D. because he lost his love's address

4. How does the poet's opinion of the pie differ from his love's opinion of the pie?

   ____

   ____

5. Write a one-sentence summary of this ballad.

   ____

   ____

Read the poem. Then, answer the questions on page 113.

Inspiration

Mrs. Kami Kaminski, the seventh-grade English teacher, had assigned her class to write a poem. "Write about something you like. Perhaps about this beautiful day. Perhaps about a sport you enjoy playing or watching. Perhaps about a person you admire or adore."

"Oh, boy!" moaned a despondent Madeline. She didn't have a clue what to choose for a poetry topic. Sitting glumly at the dining room table that evening, unable to focus on a central theme, Madeline became distracted by her baby sister.

"Hey, you little squirt! You're my inspiration!" she laughed. And away she wrote.

When Becky first did grace us with her charm,
I promised Mom I'd keep her from all harm.
I'd hold her tightly, rocking her at night
To scare away the goblins that would fright.

Then came those diapers, **noxious** with their smell.
Warm baby food ensmearing face as well
As floor, wall, me! "This babe's a creepy snake
She is!" I cried. "She's keeping me awake!"

My days are changed. Her naps **preempt** all mine.
I cringe to hear her noisy fussy whine.
Her little burp smells linger on my clothes.
My chats with Mom are less than I'd have chose.

Yet anger flees. My heart cries all a'thrill
When in my arms she nestles, cuddly still.

Name________________________________

Poetry

Use the poem on page 112 to answer the questions. Cite evidence from the text to support your answer.

1. What is Madeline's assignment?

____

2. Why can't she begin it immediately?

____

3. What does she choose as her topic and why?

____

4. What does Madeline like most about her sister?

____

5. What are four things Madeline dislikes about her sister?

____

6. What promise did she make to her mother? What is noble about this promise?

____

7. What does *noxious* mean?

____

8. What does *preempt* mean?

____

9. What is the theme of this poem?

____

10. What poetry elements does Madeline use in her poem? Give examples.

____

11. How does Madeline structure her poem? What does this help the reader to understand about how she feels about her sister?

____

____

Name________________________________

Read the poem. Then, answer the questions on page 115.

If You Were Coming in the Fall

If you were coming in the Fall,
I'd brush the Summer by
With half a smile, and half a spurn,
As housewives do a fly.

If I could see you in a year,
I'd wind the months in balls,
And put them each in separate drawers
For fear the numbers fuse.

If only centuries delayed,
I'd count them on my hand,
Subtracting, till my fingers dropped
Into Van Dieman's Land.

If certain, when this life was out
That yours and mine should be,
I'd toss it yonder, like a rind,
And take Eternity.

But now, uncertain of the length
Of this, that is between,
It goads me, like the goblin bee,
That will not state its sting.

by Emily Dickinson

Name________________________________

Use the poem on page 114 to answer the questions.

1. What is the main conflict in the poem?

   A. The speaker does not know what day or year it is.

   B. The speaker does not know when she will see her love again.

   C. The speaker is being stung by bees.

   D. The speaker is confused by the passing of time.

2. What does the speaker say is her main worry?

   A. She will count time until her fingers drop off.

   B. She would rather die than not see her love again.

   C. She is "uncertain of the length" of time until she sees her love again.

   D. She is haunted by goblin bees.

3. Which one of these is a metaphor used in the poem? Check the poem for the exact wording.

   A. comparing the summer to a housefly

   B. comparing the months to balls of yarn

   C. comparing death to eternity

   D. comparing a year to a chest of drawers

4. Which one of these is a simile used in the poem? Check the poem for the exact wording.

   A. comparing eternity to the rind of an orange

   B. comparing the summer to a housefly

   C. comparing months to balls of yarn

   D. comparing a year to a chest of drawers

5. Which of these is a good summary of the poem and its conflict?

   A. The speaker could easily cope with the absence of her love if she only knew for how long she had to wait.

   B. The speaker feels stung by the absence of her love because he never said goodbye.

   C. The speaker misses her love and counts the days until she sees him again.

   D. The speaker is afraid she will never see her love again.

6. This poem speaks to the uncertainty and unsettled feeling of longing for a loved person. What other kind of metaphors or similes could the poet have used to describe this feeling?

   ____

   ____

   ____

Name________________________________

Poetry

Read the poem. Then, answer the questions.

Three Haiku by Basho

(1) At the ancient pond
a green frog plunges into
the sound of water.

(2) Come outdoors to view
the truth of flowers blooming
amid poverty.

(3) Sick on my journey,
only my dreams will wander
these desolate moors.

1. What makes these three poems haiku?

   A. They are stories of journeys made by Japanese poets.

   B. They have a specific syllable pattern and offer insights through aspects of nature.

   C. They are lyrical poems about tragedy and loss.

   D. They have topics based on true historical events.

2. What is the pattern of haiku?

   A. first line: seven syllables; second line: five syllables; third line: five syllables

   B. first line: five syllables; second line: five syllables; third line: seven syllables

   C. first line: five syllables; second line: seven syllables; third line: five syllables

   D. first line: seven syllables; second line: seven syllables; third line: five syllables

3. What is the theme of haiku number 2?

   A. Frogs dive into the sound of water, not water itself.

   B. Even in poverty, people can take comfort in the beauty of nature.

   C. Flowers are truthful and honest.

   D. The moors are sad and lonely.

4. What happens in haiku number 3?

   A. The poet is ill and cannot hike across the moors.

   B. The poet sees flowers and takes heart in their beauty.

   C. The poet hikes across the moors and then becomes ill.

   D. The poet dreams that he becomes ill on a journey.

Name________________________________

Read the passage. Then, complete the activity.

Rhyme Schemes

Poetry discusses feelings, ideas, or events. Sometimes a poem recounts a tale from history or legend. Other times, a poem presents a simple image that symbolizes an emotion or captures one moment in time. Some poems do not rhyme, but some do. Poems that do rhyme have identifiable *rhyme schemes*. The rhyme scheme is identified by using alphabet letters to identify the pairs of lines that rhyme. Sometimes these rhyming lines are together, and sometimes they are separated.

Here is an example:

a A timeless tree stood
b on the edge of a dream.
a And thought that it could
b run like the stream.

Because *stood* and *could* rhyme, the lines that end in those words are marked with an **a**. *Dream* and *stream* rhyme, so the lines that end in those words are marked with a **b**.

Match the missing words to each stanza to complete the rhyme schemes.

_____ 1. City noises, crowded street;
Country sun, rows of ________.

_____ 2. In an alley, a flower grows.
It stands alone, an upturned bell.
How did it get there? The wind knows,
A secret it will never ________.

_____ 3. A shower of tears rains down on the ________.
This mountain and I are both soaked to the bone.

_____ 4. As she walked along the ________,
She found some shells but wanted more.

_____ 5. My loyal dog, a noble friend,
Has sadly met his mortal ________.

A. tell
B. shore
C. end
D. stone
E. wheat

6. How does rhyme scheme impact a poem?

____

____

Name________________________________

Read the poem. Then, answer the questions.

Pebble Rings, Like Memories

The old stone bridge across Rügen Bay
Is one of my favorite places to play.
I toss pebbles for Mom, and a pebble for Dad,
And a rock for the horses and chickens we had.
I watch as each of the stones makes rings
Like the song that each of my memories sings.
For my wife—for my dear and precious Lenore—
My hands and my eyes throw several more.
And then, before my playing is done
I throw the most important one,
For the memory of my son.

by Robert Hatfield

1. What makes this poem an elegy? How does this structure contribute to the meaning of the poem?

____

____

2. Write one example of a simile from the poem. What does it mean?

____

3. Write two pairs of rhyming words from the poem.

____

4. How old does the speaker seem at the end of the poem?

____

5. Is the speaker happy or sad? How do you know?

____

6. What is the theme of this poem?

____

Name________________________________

Read the poem. Then, answer the questions.

We Crouch in Caves

We crouch in caves of dirt and coal,
Our bodies stiff and fingers wrapped with tape.
This place is an endless ebony tunnel.
With counted beats, our muscles strong and tight
Chip away at walls of rock.
Faster now to fight the clock,
The air resounds with the sound of picks;
With steady rhythm in our souls,
We work in pairs, my dad and I.
We dream secret dreams
Until the whistle leaves us spent but done.

by Elaine Dion

1. Write a short summary of this poem. What is the poem about?

____

____

2. What metaphor appears in this poem?

____

3. What does the poet mean by "we dream secret dreams"?

____

____

4. Who are the two people described in the poem?

____

____

5. How would you describe the tone of this poem?

____

____

Answer Key

Page 5

1. Bullying is a problem in schools. 2. verbal, social, physical; 3. To inform, the author gives facts about bullying and helps readers understand that it is never okay.

Page 7

1. The kids hang together, but leave Josh out. 2. The kids force Josh to leave. 3. This group attitude toward Josh seems to be a bad idea. 4. Mark: thoughtful; other students: followers; Nick: bully; Joshua: isolated; 5. Answers will vary. 6. Answers will vary but should include that one discusses facts and is an informational text while the other discusses someone's personal response to a peer being bullied and is a fictional portrayal. Both passages deal with bullying. 7. The author has Mark consider how he may be making Josh feel and understand his actions and the actions of his peers are wrong.

Page 9

1. Manners for mealtimes have changed over time. 2. C; 3. B; 4. A; 5. D; 6. A; 7. E; 8. B; 9. C

Page 11

1. Mia has manners that her parents don't agree with. 2. At the end, she thinks about correcting her parents to justify her eating habits. 3. They stare at her and reprimand her. 4. Yes. She says she knows if she argues the point, they will think she is a know-it-all, and she apologizes. 5. Answers will vary but should include that one discusses facts and is an informational text while the other discusses Mia's personal response to perceived manners and is a fictional portrayal. Both passages focus on mealtime manners. 6. The author uses Mia's fictional encounter with her parents to teach facts about the history of dining manners.
7. Answers will vary.

Page 13

1. C; 2. C; 3. D; 4. A; 5. D; 6. A; 7. Stories will vary.

Page 15

1. Answers will vary but should indicate that the article is about lightning: what it is, and how it affects people. 2. students, science fans, or people interested in weather facts; 3. Because Franklin is a familiar historical personage and creates an instant mental image. 4. Yes. Examples will vary. 5. to tie the conclusion back to the introduction, which features Benjamin Franklin and his kite; 6. to inform and educate readers so they can use the safety tips themselves; 7. less than 1 in 2.5 million

Page 17

1. They weren't allowed to ask their masters, no records were kept, and they did not know of months or days. 2. He lived with his grandparents away from the other slaves. 3. the ladder; 4. His grandfather was a free man. His grandmother was a slave. 5. 1817; 6. The author begins by discussing the relationship between slaves and masters, and then discusses the living conditions and

Answer Key

the relationship with his family. This helps the reader to understand the circumstances in which the author grew up. 7. The work is written in first person.

Page 19

1. They wanted to be with their husbands or brothers, they wanted to fight to free the slaves or protect the Confederacy, or they wanted adventure. 2. She sent it home to her family. 3. She wrote about battles and marches, the weather in the south, and her bravery. 4. Her great-nephew found her letters. 5. The author says Wakeman was a brave woman. 6. Answers will vary but should include the main events of Wakeman's life.

Page 21

1. To inform readers about unique hotels. 2. swinging monkeys; 3. Room service would dive to your room and bring the pizza in a watertight container. 4. a small container or case; 5. It is made of ice and snow, even the beds. It melts every spring and is rebuilt every fall. 6. Answers will vary.

Page 23

1. X; 2. S; 3. S; 4. X; 5. X; 6. S; 7. S; 8. S; 9. X; 10. S; 11. Answers will vary but should include a simile.

Page 24

1. Her village has been destroyed. 2. She doesn't like them. She says she is angry and full of fury because of the storm. 3. She feels guilty because she is relieved she wasn't there for the storm. 4. Answers will vary but should include that one discusses facts and is an informational text while the other discusses someone's personal response to the storm and is a fictional portrayal. Both passages discuss tsunamis and their effects. 5. Answers will vary.

Page 25

1. Animals have cultures that impact their way of life. 2. No, the passage says "scientists are discovering that animals have culture, too," meaning they are in the process of gaining this knowledge and have not always known. 3. They learn it. 4. The purpose of culture in animals is to help them to relate to each other and to be able to survive. Answers will vary. Check students' highlighting.

Page 27

1. B; 2. A; 3. D; 4. B; 5. Answers will vary but should include a reference to this being the first modern media coverage of a war.

Page 29

1. B; 2. E; 3. A; 4. C; 5. D; 6. F; 7. Answers will vary.

Page 31

1. after grandmother passed away; 2. She loses her grandmother and has to move, leaving her home and friends. 3. At first she doesn't want to leave, but after talking with her mother, she understands she needs to leave because it is what's best for her family and she needs to have hope for their future. 4. She is brave and strong. Even though she doesn't want to go, she knows she has to be brave, so she changes her perspective.

Answer Key

5. uneasy or fearful; 6. She has heard stories about what happens on the ships. 7. Answers will vary but should include that one discusses facts and is an informational text while the other discusses a character's personal response to the famine and is a fictional portrayal. Both passages discuss the potato famine and how it affected peoples' lives. 8. Answers will vary.

Page 33

1. because it is wider in the middle than at the ends, making it both buoyant and stable; 2. Answers will vary. 3. Dugout: made using controlled fire, paddled by two people, used by the Arawak, made from a tree; Both: are types of canoes, waterproof, stable water transportation; Kayak: made from a wood or bone frame, paddled by one person, used by the Inuit

Page 35

1. B; 2. A; 3. C; 4. B; 5. At first Kelly envied Shauna. The author shows this by the way Kelly admired Shauna's clothes and hair. By the end, she realized Shauna was lonely. She would have to eat dinner by herself again and be all alone in her big house again.

Page 37

1. animal lover, meteorologist, losing pitcher, cobra owner, all-state slugger; 2. Report 1: weather; Report 2: deaths; Report 3: sports; 3. Report 1: scorcher, meteorologist; Report 2: tabby, sensitive; Report 3: thrice, contest or slugfest

Page 39

1. television; 2. Answers will vary but may include willpower or spunk. 3. It's up to the parents if they want their child to watch. 4. He can't find anything that interests him. 5. The story of the tsunami because he had been interested in the nation of China since the fifth grade. 6. The story of the disaster is too sad and graphic for him to watch. 7. He's not motivated. He doesn't really enjoy watching the television, but he's not motivated to do anything else. Check students' highlighting.

Page 40

1. toddlers: 2 hours, school age children: 4 hours; 2. To inform readers of the benefits and drawbacks of television. 3. It can be informational and educational. 4. It can take away from exercise and family time. 5. Answers will vary but should include that one discusses facts and is an informational text while the other discusses someone's personal response to television and is a fictional portrayal. They both are concerned with watching too much TV.

Page 41

Answers will vary based on survey data.

Page 43

1. He broke Mama's favorite dish. 2. his tears, to show how much the little boy was crying; 3. to not draw attention and to hold the pain inside; 4. She is disappointed. 5. She holds him and comforts him. 6. a. missive; b. comforter; c. plunked; Check students' highlighting.

Answer Key

Page 45
1. Answers will vary but may include thoughtful, concerned, honest. 2. how he could help the hungry and poor; 3. They will continue to beg, fail to help society, and children will be forced to beg. No. 4. They don't eat all of their meals, and they don't appreciate the comforts they have. 5. The setting makes him question his morals and the morals of those around him, as well as how poor people are treated. Check students' highlighting.

Page 47
1. American Indians of the Great Plains; 2. bison; 3. poor weapons and unmatched speed; 4. using the skins of animals; 5. hunters; 6. Horses made travel easier and they had better tools for hunting. 7. thunderous, boisterous; 8. grooves; 9. scent; Check students' highlighting.

Page 48
1. She petted them, let the python curl around her neck, and swam with the wood duck. 2. The lynx, because it was in a bad mood. 3. Patsy takes a trip to the zoo. This idea is developed as the author describes her visit to each of the pods. 4. Answers will vary. Check students' highlighting.

Page 49
1. Chrissie Foster; 2. a granola bar; 3. 2 hr. 20 min; 4. his dog; 5. caterpillar diseases; 6. the All-Flakes Bowl Inn; 7. 45 min; 8. his Anthropology class; 9. 10 min; 10. 12:37; Check students' highlighting.

Page 50
1. 1968 Lolich Lane; 2. 6; 3. the president of *Sports Freaks*; 4. no; 5. so the lawn service can have access to the grounds and work; 6. $1,200; 7. Perry Walsh; 8. 24 weeks; 9. Monday or Tuesday; Check students' highlighting.

Page 51
1. Both studies showed it is beneficial to dream because dreams help you remember new information. 2. The hippocampus helps you remember the past and stores memories. 3. Dr. Robert Stickgold; 4. two-thirds; Check students' highlighting.

Page 53
1. F; 2. F; 3. O; 4. F; 5. O; 6. F; 7. F; 8. F; 9. O; 10. O; 11. Scientists can study plants and animals and discover how living things interacted with each other many years ago. 12. It was once known for its decorative uses, but now it is known for its scientific uses.

Page 55
1. F; 2. F; 3. O; 4. F; 5. F; 6. O; 7. F; 8. F; 9. O; 10. F; 11. F; 12. O; 13. O; 14. F; 15. O

Page 57
1. Hawaii; 2. less than 2 months; 3. summer exchange student; 4. girl; 5. biology; 6. exotic bird or parrot; 7. Japan; 8. Toronto, Ontario; 9. soccer; 10. visiting the volcano and playing sports

Page 59
1. a mystic; 2. They can speak to the trees. 3. 7; 4. At her order, trees captured the enemy. 5. He may want to use her for her powers. 6. pertaining to trees; 7. Answers will vary. They were merely servants, her enemies

Answer Key

only because of their masters. 8. autumn

Page 60
1. bat; 2. spider; 3. duck; 4. moth; 5. frog; 6. opossum; 7. rabbit; 8. ant; 9. hummingbird; 10. monarch butterfly; 11. blue racer; 12. pike

Page 61
1. E; 2. C; 3. G; 4. B; 5. A; 6. D; 7. F

Page 63
1. from the point of view of the letter writer, a young soldier; first person; 2. Answers will vary but may include young, opinionated, and lonely. 3. He says they fought bravely and calls them heroic. 4. He calls them turncoats and says Lenin has things "under his thumb." 5. Answers will vary.

Page 65
1. A; 2. B; 3. B; 4. A; 5. A; 6. B; 7. A; 8. C

Page 67
1. a. quickly; b. dangerously; c. yell loudly; d. small enclosure; e. anything you could imagine; f. transport; g. high-pitched little kids; h. sped; i. metal bolt; j. villainous; k. open wide; 2. The narrator sees it as an exciting adventure. This is shown by "oh it was fun!" and "we had the ride of our lives." 3. surprised and perhaps frightened

Page 68
1. E; 2. G; 3. I; 4. A; 5. B; 6. J; 7. F; 8. C; 9. D; 10. K; 11. H; 12; L

Page 69
1. A; 2. A; 3. B; 4. B; 5. A; 6. B; 7. B; 8. A

Page 70
1. shut; 2. stretch; 3. Gretel; 4. foot; 5. Indian; 6. dance; 7. *Odyssey*; 8. goats; 9. eggs; 10. south; 11. Eve; 12. roll; 13. cheese; 14. fall; 15. doom; 16. winter; 17. Q's; 18. repel; 19. conquer; 20. tell; 21. Clark; 22. fro; 23. subtract; 24. jelly; 25. there; 26. saucer

Page 71
1. C; 2. B; 3. B; 4. A; 5. D; 6. B; 7. A; 8. B; 9. A

Page 72
1. B; 2. C; 3. A; 4. B; 5. D; 6. B; 7. D; 8. C; 9. A

Page 73
1. D; 2. B; 3. B; 4. D; 5. A; 6. A

Page 74
1. D; 2. F; 3. H; 4. A; 5. G; 6. B; 7. C; 8. E; 9. I

Page 75
1. fly; 2. seas; 3. birds; 4. vast; 5. across; 6. silently; Birds silently fly across vast seas. 7. climbed; 8. obedient; 9. old; 10. cautiously; 11. creaky; 12. pews; 13. children; Cautiously obedient children climbed creaky old pews. 14. stout; 15. resolutely; 16. hauled; 17. cartons; 18. laborers; 19. 144; 20. refrigerator; 144 stout laborers hauled refrigerator cartons resolutely.

Page 76
1. clarinet; 2. Hansel; 3. plover; 4. align; 5. bone; 6. follow; 7. football; 8. fifth; 9. Macbeth; 10. bowl; 11. Lisbon; 12. island; 13. squid; *The Call of the Wild*; Challenge: Jack London

Answer Key

Page 77
1. injure; 2. cumbersome; 3. concrete; 4. deadlock; 5. wrangle; 6. reference; 7. whirlwinds; 8. hygiene; 9. bacteria; 10. nocturnal; 11. excessive; 12. security

Page 78
1. clarinet; 2. lips; 3. horrendous; 4. baton; 5. brought; 6. awful; 7. beet; 8. class; 9. musical; 10.smiled

Page 79
1. bistro; 2. mirth; 3. adventures; 4. investigator; 5. flicker; 6. turret; 7. palpitate; 8. detritus; 9. mass; 10. pretentious; 11. demise; 12. carafe; 13. andante; 14. gentleman; 15. rust; 16. jade; 17. bellowing; 18. repel

Page 80
1. underestimated; 2. stripes; 3. metal detectors; 4. unparalleled; 5. distinguished; 6. milestone; 7. interacting; 8. preparedness; 9. city

Page 81
1. walk; 2. kindle; 3. polish; 4. whimper; 5. harmonize; 6. examine; 7. comprehend; 8. sneeze; 9. share; 10. heckle; 11. grimace; 12. sparkle; 13. tighten

Page 82
1. June; 2. Movers; 3. appreciate; 4. Steinway; 5. slogan; 6. complaints; 7. finely; 8. gouged; 9. entrance; 10. neighboring; 11. slid; 12. in; 13. repair; 14. Cost; 15. haste; 17. apparently; 18. inside; 19. civilly; 20. contact

Page 83
tropical punch, 1; lemonade, 1; orange-pineapple drink, 1; dried beef, 1; shrimp cocktail, 1; carrot sticks, 1; peach ambrosia, 1; beef steak, 3; macaroni and cheese, 2; potatoes au gratin, 1; broccoli au gratin, 1; green beans with mushrooms, 1; green beans and broccoli, 1; butter cookies, 1; chocolate pudding, 1; tapioca pudding, 1; candy-coated peanuts, 3

Page 84
1. After the presentation, more students said they would wear a helmet. Before the presentation, more people said they would ride on the handlebars or with two people on a bike. 2. Her report influenced her classmates. 3. the statistics about bicycle-related injuries and deaths

Page 85
1. Em; 2. Hal, Garth; 3. snow; 4. Bob and Em; 5. Chloe, Dot, and Em; 6. 10 cm; 7. only month with more hail than snow; 8. 75 cm; 9. 62 cm; 10. Dot, Chloe, Em, Bob, Alf, Fern, Irma, Garth, Hal

Page 87
1. Answers will vary but should include information about the treatment of factory workers. 2. The conditions of sweatshops need to be changed. People are working in cold, crowded conditions. People are working 12 hours a day. There is poor sanitation and ventilation. 3. He asks the readers to speak with factory owners, start rallies or ask others to do so, donate money, and anything else they can think of to correct the injustices he has described.

Answer Key

4. The factory owners might fight back and things might get worse. 5. The author lets the reader know there is a difference between his point of view and the factory owners' point of view by saying if readers do nothing, they unite themselves with the people who run the factories. 6. Answers will vary.

Page 89
1. B; 2. C; 3. B; 4. D; 5. B

Page 91
1. blue, calm, to feel cool; 2. red, love and passion, to increase heart rate; 3. green, nature and healing, to decorate hospital rooms; 4. black, death and evil, mourning clothes; 5. purple, royalty, to stimulate creativity and intuition; 6. Answers will vary. 7. relaxation and depression; 8. Answers will vary. 9. It speeds up breathing and increases the heart beat. 10. The author organizes the passage by beginning with the idea that colors represent different feelings and reactions. From there, each paragraph is used to describe a different color and its specifics.

Page 92
1. D; 2. A; 3. B; 4. C; 5. B; 6. C; 7. D; 8. A; 9. D; 10. B; 11. C; 12. A

Page 93
Aaron: 13, Becca: 12, Harry: 10

Page 94
1.

	fraction	$	-$4	+1/2$	new total
first	1/2	30	26	+13	$39.00
second	3/10	18	14	+7	$21.00
third	1/5	12	8	+4	$12.00

2. cedar, spruce, larch, hemlock, pine;
3. Robert-grandfather, Bob-mother, Rob-son

Page 95
1. Andrew, Holly, soda; 2. Bill, Ivy, pretzels; 3. Chase, Ginny, cookies; 4. Dion, Felicia, chips; 5. Edgar, Jan, carrots/celery

Page 96
1. Answers will vary but may include pets can eat or trample plants, fight, or injure wildlife, and spread diseases to other animals.
2. Answers will vary but may include that pets can bite other park visitors. 3. Answers will vary but may include pets might get lost, eat poisonous plants or be attacked by other animals. 4. possible; 5. possible

Page 97
1. Ben Daniels and Shannon Shaw; 2. The farmer claims that his chickens are raising insects for food. 3. North Dakota, last Thursday; 4. They build pens with their beaks, coordinate community goals, and plan insect harvests. 5. "some folks around here"

Page 99
1. B; 2. D; 3. C; 4. D; 5. To create a strong visual picture of the setting.

Answer Key

Page 101

1. The story takes place on the seacoast at night. This adds to Lee's fear for the danger Chang might be in. 2. Lee and her brother Chang; 3. A fisherman's young sister fears that he has been lost in a storm. 4. She tries to light a lamp for Chang, but the wind blows out her matches. She then blows a whistle, but loses it in the sea. She calls out her brother's name but the wind is too noisy. 5. She sees a light on the horizon and knows it's Chang. 6. Lee hears Chang calling to her. 7. personification: The wind is blowing so strongly it sounds like sobbing. 8. It is implied that Lee has no family except Chang. Answers will vary but may include a family friend could take care of Lee.

Page 103

1. the classroom and the speaker's home; It helps us to see the speaker's excitement and everything she is looking forward to.
2. Answers will vary but should include specific information from the story.
3. December; The narrator talks about the vacation and gifts. 4. Answers will vary but should mention some specific outdoor activities. 5. Chart answers will vary. Some possible answers include: sight—gray clouds and brown-tiled lobby; sound—rustling of wrapping paper and shrill bell; taste—salty pretzels and tart punch; smell—scent of vanilla and scent of almonds; touch—silky scarf and cold windowpane

Page 105

Characters: Aaron and his cousin (the narrator); Setting: spring in northern Minnesota; Story Map: events of the story should be in chronological order. By the end of the story, Aaron begins to treat the narrator like a friend instead of a younger cousin.

Page 107

1. B; 2. B; 3. C; 4. D; 5. A; 6. Firewood heats the dining room. Water for the garden comes from a well. 7. Answers will vary.

Page 109

1. Answers will vary but could include fearful, experienced seaman, religious, or worried. 2. sea monsters and that his ship will sail off the edge of the world; 3. From the names of the ships, it is clear that this is Columbus' expedition of 1492. 4. They were signs that land was nearby; the wood had not been in the water long and the birds needed to rest on land at night. 5. They try to scare each other with stories of monsters and sea creatures. 6. Answers will vary.

Page 110

Scene 1: 4, 2 ,7, 1, 5, 3, 6; Scene 2: 6, 3, 4, 1, 7, 5, 2

Page 111

1. B; 2. D; 3. B; 4. The poet likes the pie, but his love does not. It is so spicy that she runs away. 5. Answers will vary.

Page 113

1. to write a poem; 2. No topic came to mind. 3. her baby sister, because she is right there; 4. holding her in her arms; 5. smelly diapers, messy food, can't sleep, fussy, and burp smells; 6. to take care of her sister; She does it in spite of things she doesn't like. 7. poisonous; toxic; 8. to come before,

Answer Key

to be more important than; 9. Even though siblings may annoy us, we still love them. 10. rhyme and imagery; examples: charm, harm, warm baby food, smelly diapers; 11. She begins by telling about the arrival of her baby sister, then tells all of the things that annoy her, and ends by telling the reader that none of the bad things matter because she really loves her sister.

Page 115
1. B; 2. C; 3. B; 4. B; 5. A; 6. Answers will vary.

Page 116
1. B; 2. C; 3. B; 4. A.

Page 117
1. E; 2. A; 3. D; 4. B; 5. C; 6. It can give the poem a certain rhythm and help to create imagery.

Page 118
1. It expresses grief for something lost. This structure helps the reader understand the speaker's loss for his loved ones. 2. *Like the song that each of my memories sings;* He is comparing the rings to his memories. 3. Rings/sings (or any ending from a couplet pair); 4. an older (middle-aged to elderly) man; 5. sad for the death of his son, wife, parents, and his lost youth; 6. remembering loved ones

Page 119
1. Answers will vary but should indicate it is about a father and child working in a coal mine. 2. *This place is an endless ebony tunnel.* 3. Answers will vary but should indicate that the miners are longing to be elsewhere or lost in other thoughts as they work. 4. A father and his child. 5. Answers will vary; this poem can have several interpretations as to tone.

Notes